CONSPIRACIES

CONSPIRACIES

HISTORY'S GREATEST PLOTS, COLLUSIONS AND COVER-UPS

CHARLOTTE GREIG

with contributions from
Nigel Cawthorne

ARCTURUS

ARCTURUS

This edition published in 2020 by Arcturus Publishing Limited
26/27 Bickels Yard, 151–153 Bermondsey Street,
London SE1 3HA

ISBN: 978-1-83857-096-5
AD008193UK

Printed in Singapore

CONTENTS

INTRODUCTION

Post 9/11, we are in a golden age of the conspiracy theory. Nowadays, it's not just crazed loners who spend too much time on the internet discussing why the NSA is gathering all that digital information on every US citizen, or whether the Russians helped Donald Trump get elected, or even why George Bush carried on reading a children's story after being told the first plane had hit the World Trade Centre.

Often enough, yesterday's conspiracy theory is today's accepted history. If you'd said at the time that Hitler started the Reichstag Fire himself to smear his Communist opposition you'd have been called paranoid. Now it's an accepted fact. And how many people today really believe that JFK was assassinated by Lee Harvey Oswald acting all alone? And are we wrong to see conspiracies in the links between, say, the US government and Halliburton or Enron? Or naïve not to?

Of course, not all conspiracy theories have a basis in fact. Some are outlandish, such as the theory that the world is hollow and inhabited at the centre; others, such as the notion that the government is hushing up alien visitations here, there and everywhere, seem like the stuff of *X-Files* episodes. Yet all of them, even the most bizarre, address facts that cannot easily be explained, or point to our psychological need to find a reason for everything that takes place in our world.

Then there are those conspiracy theories that hover entertainingly on the edge of possibility: for example, the idea that the moon landings were faked up in a film studio. And, of course, there's not a celebrity death without its attendant conspiracy theory. Was Diana murdered? Was the FBI really behind John Lennon's murder? To some, these theories simply demonstrate our human tendency to deny death and loss, to let our idols go; to others, they reveal the sinister currents of money and power that run below the public life of any celebrated figure in our culture today.

This book gathers together more than thirty of the most compelling conspiracies: ranging from the genuinely credible to the frankly implausible, from mind control conspiracies to crop circles, from WikiLeaks and the death of Alexander Litvinenko to the Holy Grail. Was Pearl Harbor a set-up? Was Marilyn Monroe murdered? We may not have the answers, but we've got some pretty good theories!

What is a conspiracy theory?

The word "conspiracy" comes from the Latin *conspirare*. Literally it means "to breathe together". In practice, it refers to two or more people making a plan of action that other parties are not told about. Theoretically that plan could be either good or bad, but over the centuries it has gained a distinctly negative sense. You can see this clearly from the way in which the word is used in the legal sphere: "conspiracy" in a legal sense always refers to wrongdoing.

Conspiracies are not by definition secret, but as the word has attached itself to criminal behaviour that's almost inevitably a part of the package. So, over the years, secrecy has become a part of our conventional sense of what a conspiracy is. And it's a crucial part when it comes to the development of conspiracy theories. Essentially, conspiracy theories are alternative explanations of history or of the world about us. Conspiracy theories suggest that dramatic events happen not by accident or for apparent reasons, but because of plans made in secrecy.

There's no doubt that conspiracy theories have been with us for thousands of years. After all, conspiracies certainly have. Whether it's the ancient Greeks conspiring to take over Troy or the Caesar's rivals conspiring to assassinate him, history is full of dramatic conspiracies. And there have always been people with a suspicious cast of mind who've come up with conspiracy theories to explain such events.

However, it's only in the past hundred years or so that conspiracy theories have really come to the fore. Perhaps that has something to do with the decline of religion. In the past people tended to see inexplicable events as the work of the Almighty. In our more secular times, however, people tend to look for the nefarious hand of man.

The late nineteenth century saw the birth of some enduring conspiracy theories. As the world was changing fast through industrialization, and the old certainties of life were being shattered, many people started to suspect that there was some powerful organization controlling all this, some group who were effectively setting themselves up as rivals to God. The prime candidates for this role, in a Europe in which anti-Semitism had long been rife, were the Jewish communities. The idea of an international Jewish conspiracy began to gain credence, especially in Russia in the turbulent years leading up to the First World War. Other candidates for the role of secret rulers of the world included the Freemasons, the Communists, and the semi-mythical group known as the Illuminati.

Such visions of a world controlled by a small and sinister cabal are still a popular element in conspiracy theories today. In fact, they lie behind almost every conspiracy theory there is. So perhaps the answer to the question "what is a conspiracy theory?" should be "it's a theory which suggests that the great world events are not what they seem; rather, they are the manifestations of a world controlled by a secret elite."

Conspiracy theories today

There has been an explosion of interest in conspiracy theories in recent years. There are many possible reasons for this – loss of faith in religion, as mentioned above, loss of faith in politicians, a sensationalist mass media that likes to broadcast sensational theories, the influence of films and novels espousing conspiracies, and so on. One major factor is undoubtedly the growth of the internet. The internet is the perfect medium for spreading conspiracy theories. Where once a rumour would be passed around a chosen few insiders and spread slowly through the metropolitan grapevine – for example the one about the identity of the Watergate source known as "Deep Throat" – these days, it will be on the internet in minutes and instantly transmitted around the world.

Thus today, when a major event occurs – take 9/11 for example – conspiracy theories immediately start to circulate on the internet. Evidence that the authorities would prefer to have kept quiet is now available to be discussed and interpreted from America to Australia. The trouble is, of course, that so too are lies, fabrications, and delusions. The internet is at once a marvellous tool for avoiding censorship and allowing the voice of truth to emerge, and also a forum in which every lunatic and partisan commentator can have their say in the era of "fake news". Today, when so many conspiracy theories appear on the internet, it is sometimes a difficult business to determine which ones are worthy of serious consideration and which are simply hearsay.

This dilemma has never been clearer than when dealing with the events of 9/11 and the subsequent war on terror. The extraordinary success of Michael Moore's documentary film

Fahrenheit 911 saw conspiracy theories go mainstream. The film takes seriously a number of conspiracy theories that might previously have been thought outlandish. As a result, audiences have been polarized. Some saw the film as irresponsible, others saw it as voicing the truths that the regular news media was scared to utter. Ultimately audience responses tended to depend on what side of the political fence the viewer happened to be sitting on. This is hardly surprising: conspiracy theories always tend to appeal to those whose political views are in opposition to those in power.

Political conspiracies

This book will attempt to offer an unbiased investigation into several aspects of state surveillance in the digital age and leave the reader to make up their own mind. We'll explore the various conspiracy theories relating to the events of 9/11. We'll try to make sense of the mysterious last moments of Flight MH370, the plane that disappeared.

We'll also look into some of the classic political mysteries of yesteryear. Did Roosevelt really let the bombing of Pearl Harbor happen in order to persuade Americans to join in World War II? And we'll consider whether Adolf Hitler could really have escaped the bunker by a secret tunnel and fled to Antarctica with Eva Braun.

Coming closer to the present, we'll examine the string of suspicious deaths and assassinations that occurred during the 1960s. The most celebrated of these, the murder of JFK, is perhaps the ultimate conspiracy theory, with endless books, films and TV programmes devoted to it. The murder of radical black American leader Malcolm X and even the death of film star Marilyn Monroe have also attracted their fair share of speculation, and we'll also discuss these cases.

Many conspiracy theories relate to the existence of Secret Societies, and we'll be looking into several of these. We'll investigate the Bilderberg Group and attempt to establish whether this shadowy group is really running our world. And who, or what, is the Illuminati? Formed in 1776, have its members, "the illuminated ones", really been the secret power behind the throne throughout modern history?

Religion has always attracted its share of conspiracy theories, too, so we'll take a tour around the strange stories that surround the Holy Grail. Could Mary Magdalen have smuggled Christianity's most precious relic out of the Holy Land and into Western Europe, where it remains hidden to this day? Closer to the present, there is the bizarre death of Roberto Calvi, nicknamed "God's banker". Could the Pope's business chiefs really have been hand in glove with the Mafia?

Stranger than fiction

And here we move onto the theories that read like the stuff of science fiction. One of the most enduring conspiracy theories of this type maintains that the moon landings were faked. Could this possibly be true? And what of extraterrestrial happenings and alien visitation? What really happened at Roswell? Or at Rendlesham Forest? And how can we explain crop circles?

Conspiracy theories, then, come in all shapes and sizes. There are those that seem to be taken from the pages of science fiction novels or thrillers. Indeed, many of them do crop up in popular fiction, not least Dan Brown's enormously popular *Da Vinci Code*, which draws from a whole tradition of Holy Grail conspiracies dating back for over a thousand years. Yet while many conspiracy theories are more entertaining than realistic, there are some that reveal genuinely disturbing information and ask important questions about secrecy in the way we are governed and receive information.

In the end it is for you, the reader, to decide which theories to believe, and which to dismiss. So prepare to enter into a world much stranger than fiction: the world of the conspiracy theory.

CHAPTER ONE:
THEY'VE GOT YOUR NUMBER

Just because they call you paranoid doesn't mean they aren't out
to get you. I mean, who can you trust these days? It's now proven
beyond reasonable doubt that countries today spend billions
spying on their own citizens, hoovering up vast quantities of
information, usually in the name of counter-terrorism. But why
did they never tell us what they were up to? And why did they wait
until troubled insiders gave the game away? Perhaps we should be
grateful to the whistle-blowers who let us in on state secrets.

DONALD TRUMP: FROM RUSSIA WITH LOVE?

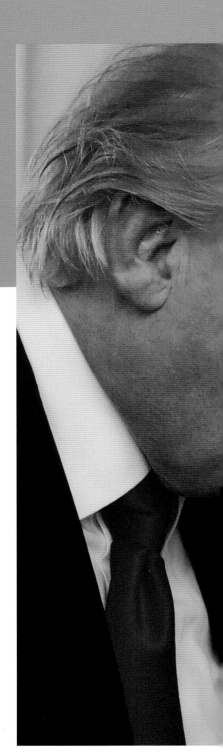

There have been repeated allegations that Russia tampered with the 2016 US presidential elections, easing Donald Trump's path to the White House. Trump denied any collusion, but senior aides have been indicted and a number pleaded guilty. As well as the Americans involved, thirteen Russian citizens and three Russian entities have been indicted by US Special Counsel, Robert Mueller.

It began when WikiLeaks published a quarter of a million diplomatic cables from Democratic hopeful Hillary Clinton's term as secretary of state provided by Chelsea – then Bradley – Manning. Then on the eve of the Democratic Convention in July 2016, WikiLeaks released emails from the Democratic National Committee that appeared to show they favoured Clinton over her rival Bernie Sanders during the primaries, implying that Clinton cheated to get the nomination.

Cybersecurity experts quickly concluded that the Russians had hacked the DNC. Bob Gourley, former Chief of Technology for the Defense Intelligence Agency, said: "The software code that I have seen from the hack had all the tell-tale signs of being Russian, including code re-used from other attacks. This is a really big deal."

Allegations of collusion do not appear to dampen personal relations as Trump chats with Russia's President Vladimir Putin at a summit on 11 November 2017.

The security firm Crowstrike, who had previously investigated hacks at the White House, the Pentagon and the State Department, also concluded that the DNC hacks were carried out by the Russians. It found that there were "two separate Russian intelligence-affiliated adversaries present in the DNC network". Trump refused to accept this. Instead, he invited Russian hackers to target Hillary Clinton's controversial personal email server, saying: "Russia, if you're listening, I hope you're able to find the thirty-thousand emails that are missing."

In September 2016, the US intelligence community unanimously accused Russia of being behind the hacking of the DNC. But Trump remained bullish, saying it "could be Russia... it could also be... somebody sitting on their bed that weighs four-hundred pounds".

Cash for favours?

Trump's then campaign manager Paul Manafort was accused of accepting millions of dollars in cash for representing Russian interests, including dealings with an oligarch with close ties to Russian President Vladimir Putin. While Manafort was running the campaign, the Republican Party changed the language in its manifesto regarding the conflict in Ukraine, removing anti-Russian sentiments.

A week before the election there was another leak, this time concerning a report handed to the FBI. The report, using Russian sources, said that the Putin regime had been supporting Trump for at least five years. It claimed that Russian intelligence had compromised Trump during his visits to Moscow and could blackmail him. However, the initial research, carried out by former MI6 officer Christopher Steele, had been funded by the Clinton campaign who clearly had a motive to discredit the Republican candidate.

When the explosive *Access Hollywood* recording emerged of Trump's obscene remarks about women in 2005, threatening to derail his bid for the presidency, thousands more leaked Clinton emails were dumped on WikiLeaks. In December, the FBI and the Department of Homeland Security published

Amid explosive allegations over his ties to Russia, US President-elect Donald Trump answers journalists' questions during a press conference on 11 January 2017, just over a week before his inauguration.

a report of the US intelligence findings linking Russia to the hack. President Barack Obama expelled thirty-five Russian diplomats and ramped up sanctions against Russia. By then, though, President Trump had been elected.

Administration in turmoil

It was then revealed that Rex Tillerson, Trump's nominee for secretary of state, had cultivated a close relationship with the Russian leader while CEO of ExxonMobil. He was sworn in on 2 February 2017, though replaced six weeks later.

In February it was found that National Security Adviser Michael Flynn had discussed the

8 June 2017: Former FBI Director James Comey testified in front of the Senate Intelligence Committee on his past relationship with President Donald Trump, and his role in the Russian interference investigation.

lifting of Obama's sanctions on Russia with Russian Ambassador Sergey Kislyak before Trump had entered the Oval Office. Making foreign policy by a private individual is a crime. Flynn resigned after twenty-three days in office. He pleaded guilty to lying to the FBI – a felony – and agreed to co-operate with the Mueller investigation.

Attorney General Jeff Sessions was accused of lying at his confirmation hearing when he said he had had "no communications with the Russians" during the election campaign. It emerged that he too had met Ambassador Kislyak.

Two months into the Trump administration, FBI Director James Comey told the House Intelligence Committee that the bureau were investigating alleged Russian involvement in the election. He was fired. In the Oval Office, Trump told the Russian ambassador and foreign minister that firing Comey had eased "great pressure". Comey then testified to the Senate that Trump had asked him to drop the FBI investigation of Flynn, constituting obstruction of justice. The White House denied this.

It was then revealed that during the election campaign, the president's son Donald Trump Jr had met Russian lawyer Natalia Veselnitskaya at Trump Tower after being told that she had damaging material on Hillary Clinton. Manafort and the president's son-in-law, Jared Kushner, had also been at that meeting. Trump Jr had already given investigators his correspondence with Assange during the election.

Facebook's Mark Zuckerberg said he would share 3,000 Russia-linked political adverts with US investigators and Twitter said it had shut down some two hundred accounts linked to a Russian misinformation campaign.

The Mueller investigation concluded in 2019 and left the final decision about Trump's complicity in the hands of the politicians.

WIKILEAKS: BITING BACK

On 19 June 2012, WikiLeaks founder Julian Assange walked into the Ecuadorian Embassy in London and claimed political asylum. This was granted a month later. Assange was wanted on a European Arrest Warrant for alleged sexual offences in Sweden. British police guarded the embassy and Assange would be arrested and deported to Sweden if he stepped outside the door.

His fear was that the Swedes would hand him over to the United States where he risked prosecution for espionage. The leaking of sensitive US material began in November 2007 – less than a year after WikiLeaks was founded – when it published a confidential manual on the day-to-day operation of the Guantánamo Bay detention camp. This revealed that the International Committee of the Red Cross were being denied access to certain prisoners, something the US military had previously denied.

Then there were accusations that WikiLeaks was interfering in US presidential elections in 2008 when the contents of the Yahoo account of Republican vice-presidential candidate Sarah Palin appeared on the website. The account had been hacked by the hacktivist group Anonymous.

Wikileaks also released 570,000 intercepts of pager messages sent on the day of the 11 September attacks, revealing the security arrangements being made for the president and his family. So what was the true intent of the WikiLeaks organization? Its purported aim was to bring important information to the public and expose the "truth". But many accused it of being partial in what it chose to reveal, so influencing world events.

Chelsea Manning

In April 2010 WikiLeaks began publishing material supplied by Chelsea Manning. Born Bradley Edward Manning, she was a Specialist and intelligence analyst at Forward Operating

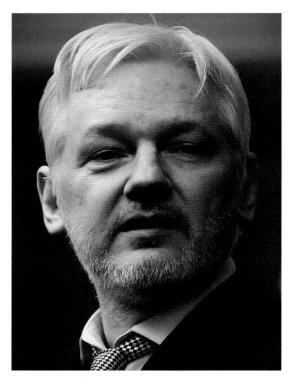

Julian Assange, the founder and editor-in-chief of WikiLeaks, is under investigation by US authorities for espionage.

Julian Assange appears at a window of the Ecuadorian Embassy in London. He would not leave the building for fear of being arrested, yet continued to influence events around the world.

Base Hammer, forty miles east of Baghdad, where she had culled hundreds of thousands of diplomatic cables and sensitive material concerning the wars in Iraq and Afghanistan. In May 2010, Manning was arrested and charged with twenty-two offences, including "aiding the enemy", a capital offence.

Manning pleaded guilty on ten of the charges and was convicted of seventeen. She was sentenced to thirty-five years. President Barack Obama commuted her sentence and she was released in 2017.

WikiLeaks published further Guantánamo Bay files in 2011, more material concerning detainees, US diplomatic and intelligence documents, and files on the war in Syria, along with material supplied by Edward Snowden on mass surveillance.

"Hostile intelligence service"

In the US, Assange could face the death penalty, or a long prison sentence, for conniving in these breaches of security. But although he was confined to a single room while the work of the Ecuadorian Embassy went on around him, Assange is thought to have influenced the outcome of the 2016 American presidential election – with the help of the Russians.

Assange made it clear that he viewed Hillary Clinton as a personal enemy. She had pushed to have him indicted after WikiLeaks published a quarter of a million diplomatic cables from her term as secretary of state provided by Manning. Emails damaging to the Clinton campaign were published by WikiLeaks at strategic intervals throughout the presidential campaign. While WikiLeaks was set up to expose conspiracies, Assange was accused of using it to participate in one himself.

In May 2017, the Swedish prosecutor dropped the investigation of the sexual misconduct charges against Assange, while in December he was granted Ecuadorian citizenship. However, in April 2019, Assange's asylum was withdrawn and the Swedish

Protesters demonstrate in support of Chelsea (then Bradley) Manning in 2013 in front of the White House. Manning was sentenced to 35 years in prison for leaking hundreds of thousands of classified documents to WikiLeaks.

authorities reopened their investigation. He was arrested and held in Belmarsh Prison. Before he left office, President Obama said that the Justice Department had determined it would be difficult to bring charges against Assange because WikiLeaks wasn't alone in publishing documents stolen by Manning. Several newspapers, including *The New York*

Hillary Clinton during her ill-fated campaign to become the first female president of the United States in 2016.

Times, did so as well and the First Amendment of the US Constitution protects the freedom of the press. However, President Donald Trump's first Director of the CIA Mike Pompeo said that WikiLeaks' activities had gone beyond those protected by the First Amendment. He said WikiLeaks "directed Chelsea Manning to intercept specific secret information, and it overwhelmingly focuses on the United States".

He called WikiLeaks "a non-state hostile intelligence service often abetted by state actors like Russia" and described founder Julian Assange as a narcissist, fraud, and coward. Attorney General Jeff Sessions confirmed that Assange's arrest was a "priority".

So is Assange a champion of transparency and free speech in the digital age, or an international conspirator with personal vendettas? His story continues to unfold. Meanwhile the Ecuadorian Embassy cut off Assange's access to the internet or social media after he tweeted about the situation in Catalonia, breaking a written promise that he made in 2017 not to interfere with the politics of other nations.

EDWARD SNOWDEN: BIG BROTHER IS WATCHING YOU

National Security Agency whistle-blower Edward Snowden revealed that America's NSA had used a top-secret "black budget" to spy on some of the US's closest allies, including France, Germany, Spain, Mexico, Brazil and even Britain, whose Government Communications Headquarters (GCHQ) operated in collaboration with the NSA under the Five Eyes agreement, along with Canada, Australia, and New Zealand. It also tapped the phones of 122 world leaders, including Angela Merkel's. Indeed, the NSA and GCHQ operated a worldwide conspiracy monitoring the phone calls, texts, and emails of countless individuals, companies, and institutions, including those of its own citizens.

Snowden joined the CIA in 2006 as a computer systems administrator at the global communications division in the agency's headquarters at Langley, Virginia. After ten months, he was posted to Geneva where he learned the tricks of the intelligence trade such as getting "targets" drunk enough to end up in jail, then bailing them out so that they would be in your debt and become informants.

In 2009, he quit the CIA and joined Dell, a major contractor to the NSA. Posted to the NSA offices at Yokota air base outside Tokyo, he taught officials and military officers how to defend their networks from hackers. There he was exposed to live NSA monitors showing targeted killings in the Middle East, watching as military and CIA

Edward Snowden, former CIA agent turned whistle-blower, has accepted asylum in Russia.

drones turned people into body parts. He also learned about the NSA's mass surveillance capabilities and their ability to map the movement of everyone in a city by monitoring their MAC addresses, a unique identifier emitted by each cell phone, computer, and electronic device.

State snooping

Three years later, he was posted to the CIA's information-sharing office in Hawaii. This was supposed to be monitoring activities in countries such as North Korea. Instead it was global exchange and he was horrified to discover that the content of communications – as well as the metadata – from millions of emails and phone calls made by Palestinian- and Arab-Americans was being handed over to the Israelis. No attempt was made to disguise their identities even though they might have had relatives living in the occupied territories who could become targets on the basis of these intercepts.

The NSA also spied on the pornography-viewing habits of political radicals in case it could be used against them. Snowden said he complained to his superiors about these illegal activities. When nothing was done, he began to download files which he would later leak to the media. He then moved on to the NSA's Threat Operations Center at Fort Meade, Maryland, where he collected more evidence of the agency's illegal surveillance.

Traitor or patriot?

Snowden said that the moment he decided to blow the whistle was when he saw the Director of National Intelligence James Clapper lie under oath to Congress. On 12 March 2013, Clapper was testifying to the Senate Select Committee on Intelligence, when Senator Ron Wyden asked him: "Does the NSA

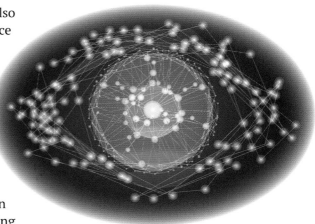

In the digital age, government monitoring of communications data is potentially without limits.

collect any type of data at all on millions, or hundreds of millions, of Americans?"

Clapper responded: "No, sir.... Not wittingly. There are cases where they could inadvertently, perhaps, collect, but not wittingly."

Snowden knew this was untrue. The NSA logged nearly every telephone call Americans make. It also bugged European Union offices in Washington and Brussels and, with GCHQ, has tapped the Continent's major fibre-optic communications cables. Thirty-eight embassies and missions were on its list of surveillance targets, including those belonging to allies such as France, Japan, and Mexico.

As an "infrastructure analyst", Snowden's job was to look for new ways to break into internet and telephone traffic around the world. This gave him access to lists of devices all over the world that the NSA had hacked. He also discovered that, as well as hoovering up staggering amounts of information, the NSA had developed cyberweapons so it could, if necessary, go on the attack. The NSA and Israel co-wrote the Stuxnet computer worm used to sabotage Iran's nuclear programme.

On the run

In May 2013, Snowden fled to Hong Kong with four laptop computers thought to contain the files he had downloaded. There he began briefing journalists. On 6 June, the *Guardian* printed a story saying that the NSA had been given permission to collect the telephone records of the millions of customers of the US telecoms giant Verizon. The order had been granted by the secret Foreign Intelligence Surveillance Court. The following day the *Guardian* and the *Washington Post* reported the NSA was accessing the systems of US internet giants including Google and Facebook, and collecting data under a clandestine surveillance programme called Prism. Since 2007, this programme had allowed the NSA to collect material including emails, live chats, and search histories. GCHQ also had access to Prism.

Then the *Guardian* revealed the existence of another programme called Boundless Informant that gave analysts summaries of the NSA's worldwide data collection activities by counting metadata. It showed that the NSA was collecting more information on Americans in the United States than on Russians in Russia despite repeated assurances to Congress that it could not keep track of all the surveillance it performs on American communications.

In the US, Snowden was branded a traitor and he was charged with espionage and theft. Offered asylum in Ecuador, he found his US passport revoked, leaving him stranded at Moscow's Sheremetyevo International Airport while changing planes there. After 39 days in the transit lounge, Snowden accepted asylum in Russia. Despite attempts to shut him up, evidence of a global conspiracy to spy on friend and foe alike, on an unprecedented scale, conducted by the NSA and GCHQ, continued to come out.

Edward Snowden speaks via videoconference to an audience at the 2014 SXSW festival in Austin, Texas.

FLIGHT MH370: THE GREAT DISAPPEARING ACT

On 8 March 2014, Malaysian Airlines Flight MH370 took off from Kuala Lumpur International Airport bound for Beijing with 239 people on board. Less than an hour into the flight, radio contact was lost and the plane vanished from air traffic controllers' radar screens. Only later was it discovered that Malaysian military radar had continued to track the plane as it veered westwards across the Malay Peninsula, then northwest up the Straits of Malacca towards the Andaman Sea.

Eventually, sophisticated analysis of the satellite communication from the plane's automated systems indicated that it had then turned southwards and the search moved to the South Indian Ocean. One piece of debris, a flaperon broken off from the wing, washed up on the French island of Réunion, some 2,500 miles west of the search area, on 29 July 2015. Since then, other small pieces of wreckage that might have come from the wings and engine of the missing aircraft have been found along the coast of east Africa where oceanographers said that currents would have carried debris from the search area. However, a search of the sea floor where the plane was supposed to have crashed, lasting three years and costing $130 million (£105m), could find no sign of the huge fuselage of the Boeing 777. And if the plane had broken up on impact how come none of the debris you would expect to float – seat cushions, life jackets, luggage, even corpses – had ended up floating in the sea?

Strange events

This has spawned all sorts of conspiracy theories – from a hijacking gone wrong to pilot suicide, an accidental shoot-down alien abduction, and even that it had been substituted for MH17, shot down over the Ukraine three months later. One of the most intriguing came from aviation expert Jeff Wise, who led CNN's coverage of the disappearance of MH370. It centred on the fact that twenty employees of Freescale Semiconductors, an avionics firm said to specialize in stealth technology, were on board.

Wise noted that the plane was initially assumed to have flown north from the Andaman Sea and Malaysian prime minister Najib Razak had appealed to the president of Kazakhstan, Nursultan Nazarbayev, formerly first secretary of the Communist Party of Kazakhstan and an ally of Vladimir Putin, to allow Malaysia to set up a search in Kazakhstan. Only later was it thought that the plane had travelled south to crash into the sea in one of the remotest spots on earth.

Re-examining the satellite data, Wise and the Independent Group, a band of like-minded aviation experts, decided that the plane had indeed flown north while bogus data had been fed to the satellite.

Checking the passenger list, he found that two Ukrainians and a Russian were on board. Little was known about them except that the Ukrainians came from Odessa, a former Soviet naval base, and the Russian's hobby was scuba-diving. He was sitting up front in business class, with the two Ukrainians further back in economy.

Wise reckons that the Russian came on to the plane with a bag of scuba gear, containing three full-face diving masks. Once the plane had reached cruising altitude and the cabin staff were looking the other way, he slipped into the electronics-and-equipment – or E/E – bay, which, on the Boeing 777,

could be accessed through a hatch at the front of the first-class cabin. From there, he could control all the systems on the plane.

First he would have cut off all communication, then plugged in portable equipment that would upload false satellite data to the system. From the E/E bay, he could depressurize the cabin while he and his two accomplices breathed oxygen through their diving masks.

Inside job

As he turned the plane to the west, the flight crew would have spotted that something was wrong. But there would have been nothing they could do about it. None of their checklists would have covered a possible hijacking from the E/E bay. The anti-hijacking lock on the cockpit door could also be controlled from there. When it was opened, two burly men wearing oxygen masks entered, giving the hijackers total control of the plane.

While the crew and passengers lapsed into unconsciousness, the plane flew across the Malay Peninsula along the Malaysian–Thai border, where it was unlikely that anyone would be looking out for a rogue aircraft. Then the plane turned again and flew up the Straits of Malacca between Thailand and Indonesia.

The disappearance of Flight MH370 remains one of the greatest mysteries in aviation history. How was it possible to evade the tracking systems of so many different authorities?

Instead of turning southwards, Wise reckons that Flight MH370 continued northwards to Kazakhstan, sending its last electronic "hand-shake" to the satellite near the Baikonur Cosmodrome in Kazakstan, which is leased by Russia to launch the rockets supplying the space station. Baikonur had a runway nearly 15,000 feet long, built to land the Buran space plane, the Soviet Union's version of the Space Shuttle, whose programme was cancelled in 1993. This is the only airstrip in the world built specifically for self-landing aeroplanes and the 777 has an auto-landing system. That meant that even someone who had no experience flying commercial aircraft could land the plane safely.

The plane truth?

However, Baikonur is in the middle of a flat, treeless plain, a difficult place to hide some-thing as big as a Boeing 777, and the hijackers would have had just ninety minutes to hide it before the sun came up. Studying satellite imagery, Wise noted that a huge building at Baikonur, which had been left to rot after the Buran project had been abandoned, had recently been demolished. Where it had been, there was now a large patch, around the size of a 777, covered with rubble where the plane could be hidden.

Wise says he can offer no motive for the hijacking. However, both during the Vietnam war and World War II, the Soviets seized American and Allied prisoners who had specialized technical knowledge. If the cabin had been repressurized after the hijackers had taken over the plane, the twenty employees of Freescale could now be producing the latest stealth cloaking systems for the Russians.

The sun rises over the launch pad at the Baikonur Cosmodrome in Kazakhstan. Could this be the final resting place of Flight MH370?

GARETH WILLIAMS: THE BODY IN THE BAG

On Monday 23 August 2010 GCHQ code-breaker Gareth Williams failed to turn up for work again at the Secret Intelligence Service, commonly known as MI6, where he had been seconded. No one had seen him for over a week.

The police were sent round to the Security Service flat in Pimlico, London – not far from the world-famous Tate Britain art gallery – where he was staying. After forcing entry, officers found his body – naked and decomposing – inside a red sports holdall. It had been padlocked from the outside, but the key was inside the bag, under William's body. There were no injuries on the body and no indications that he had struggled against an attacker, or tried to escape.

Wrapped in an enigma

The bag was in the bath, but no finger-, foot-, or palm-prints or DNA belonging to Williams were found on the rim of the bath, or on the padlock or zipper, and he was not wearing any gloves. There was no sign of a break-in and the heating in the flat had been turned up, even though it was mid-summer, which helped speed decomposition. Toxicology examinations showed no trace of alcohol or drugs and an initial post-mortem proved inconclusive. Nothing was missing from the flat and a couple seen leaving the building were soon ruled out of the investigation.

Williams' family believe that his death was linked to his work at SIS and that fingerprints, DNA, and other evidence had been wiped from the scene as part of a deliberate cover-up. Indeed, the authorities were plainly sensitive about the investigation. Foreign Secretary William Hague signed a public immunity certificate authorizing the withholding of the details of Williams' secret work and exempting officers of America's National Security Agency and the FBI that Williams had worked with from testifying at the inquest. SIS chief Sir John Sawers also met with the commissioner of the Metropolitan Police Sir Paul Stephenson to discuss how the investigation would be handled and who would head it.

The mystery deepens

As a direct result the coroner, Dr Fiona Wilcox, was critical of the police's handling of the investigation. Officers in the Met's counter-terrorism branch, SO15, whose role was to interview SIS witnesses, failed to take formal statements and withheld information from the senior investigating officer, Detective Chief Inspector Jackie Sebire.

The coroner also criticized the handling of an iPhone belonging to Williams and found in his work locker, which contained deleted

A brilliant mathematician, Gareth Williams had a promising future ahead of him, but his life was cut tragically short in the most bizarre circumstances.

images of him naked in a pair of boots. An iPhone found in his living room had recently been wiped and restored to factory settings. LGC Forensics were also criticized over DNA contamination, and the coroner's office was censured for failing to inform police officers of a second post-mortem.

Wilcox dismissed evidence of Williams' interest in bondage and cross-dressing as irrelevant. Only a tiny percentage of his internet browsing involved visiting bondage sites. Williams was naked in the bag, not dressed in women's clothing, and she condemned leaks to the media about him cross-dressing as a possible attempt "by some third party to manipulate a section of the evidence".

The idea that he had locked himself in the bag for some auto-erotic thrill was also ruled out. The coroner said that Williams was a "scrupulous risk assessor" – if he had locked himself into the bag, he would have taken a knife in with him to aid his escape.

Her conclusion was that Williams was probably alive when put in the bag but probably suffocated very soon afterwards either from CO_2 poisoning, hypercapnia, or the effects of a short-acting poison. Passing a narrative verdict (one which does not attribute a cause to a named individual), she said she was satisfied that "a third party placed the bag in the bath and on the balance of probabilities locked the bag". Therefore, again on the balance of probabilities, he had been killed unlawfully.

Scotland Yard spent another year investi-

Boris Karpichkov, a Russian double agent who defected to Britain, said that Williams had uncovered information that meant he had to be killed.

gating the case, only to re-affirm its original conclusions – that Williams was alone at the time of his death, had locked himself inside the bag and died when he could not get out again. This directly contradicted the coroner's findings and was thought extremely unlikely by experts.

Fresh claims

Allegations then surfaced that Williams had been working with the NSA tracking money siphoned out of Moscow by the Russian Mafia. Cars registered to the Russian Embassy were spotted near his Pimlico flat in the days before his body was discovered. There were indications that someone had broken in through a skylight the day after the body had been found and tampered with the evidence.

Then KGB defector Boris Karpichkov put forward another scenario. He said that Williams had discovered a Russian agent inside GCHQ after a bungled attempt to recruit him as a double agent by blackmailing him over his private life. Consequently, he had to be killed. This was done by short-lived poison injected in his ear. The heating was turned up in the flat so that traces of the toxin would break down before the body was found.

There was also speculation that the SIS might have been responsible. Fearing that Williams might be a whistle-blower, they had bumped him off. With their close co-operation with the police, this would be easy to cover up.

A red sports holdall of the type in which Gareth Williams' body was found.

ALEXANDER LITVINENKO: DEATH OF A DOUBLE AGENT

Alexander Litvinenko was a high flier in the KGB. He excelled in the Federal Security Service, or FSB, which replaced the KGB after the collapse of the Soviet Union. Through his work in counter-intelligence he met oligarch Boris Berezovsky. This did not endear him to his boss at the FSB Vladmir Putin and Litvinenko claimed he was given orders to assassinate Berezovsky. Going public, he appeared at a press conference revealing the conspiracy to kill Berezovsky and fellow dissident intelligence officer Mikhail Trepashkin. As a result, Litvinenko was dismissed from the FSB. Putin said: "I fired Litvinenko and disbanded his unit... because FSB officers should not stage press conferences. This is not their job. And they should not make internal scandals public."

Evading arrest, Litvinenko and his family fled to Turkey where he applied for asylum at the US embassy. When this was denied, he flew to the UK where he was granted asylum in 2001. Five years later, he naturalized as a British citizen.

Spy in exile

In Britain, he joined Boris Berezovsky, who had also fled to the UK, in his campaign against Putin. He also worked for MI6,

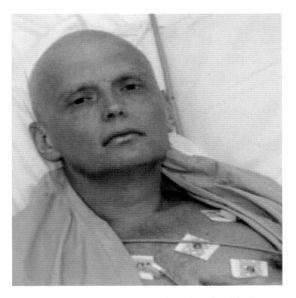

Litvinenko released a picture from his deathbed, blaming his former boss at the FSB Vladimir Putin for his demise.

though in the tradition of the service they will not confirm this. In his book *Blowing Up Russia*, Litvinenko claimed the Russian security services were complicit in a series of apartment block bombings in 1999 that killed more than three hundred people, part of a coup to bring Putin to power. He also asserted that FSB agents trained Al-Qaeda leaders in Dagestan and were involved in the 9/11 attacks. In 2002, he was convicted *in absentia* in Russia and sentenced to three and a half years for corruption, and Trepashkin, then in jail, warned him that an FSB unit had been assigned to assassinate him.

In a series of newspaper articles, Litvinenko claimed that the FSB were complicit in the 2002 Moscow theatre siege, the 2004 Beslan school massacre and numerous other terrorist attacks. According to Litvinenko, former prime minister of Italy and president of the European Commission Romano Prodi had also worked for the KGB. However, perhaps his most damaging allegation was that Vladimir Putin, by then president of the Russian Federation, had ordered the assassination of dissident journalist Anna Politkovskaya. There were wilder accusations – that Putin was involved in drug running, even that he was a paedophile.

The Millennium Hotel, where staff working in the Pine Bar tested positive for polonium-210, the isotope that killed Litvinenko.

Fateful meeting

On 1 November 2006, Litvinenko met two former KGB officers, Andrei Lugovoy and Dmitry Kovtun, in the Pine Bar of the Millennium Hotel in Mayfair. Then he had lunch with Italian nuclear-waste expert Mario Scaramella at Itsu, a sushi restaurant in Piccadilly. Afterwards he fell ill. Suffering from diarrhoea and vomiting, he found he could not walk and was taken to hospital. His throat was blistered; he could barely swallow, let alone talk. But he managed to register under the name of "Edwin Carter" and medical staff at first laughed off the suspicions he voiced until they referred the case to Scotland Yard after Litvinenko had told them who he really was. It was thought he had been poisoned with thallium. His hair fell out and a picture of him on his deathbed was released. "I want the world to see what they did to me," Litvinenko said. In a final statement, he blamed Vladimir Putin for his death.

On 22 November, Alexander Litvinenko died of heart failure. His body was later found to contain more than two hundred times the lethal dose of the radioactive element polonium. Detectives from Scotland Yard found they could trace three trails of radioactive polonium – belonging respectively to Litvinenko, Lugovoy, and Kovtun. Passengers on board the planes Lugovoy and Kovtun had flown back to Moscow with were warned to contact the Department of Health. Meanwhile the UK Atomic Weapons Establishment traced the source of the polonium to the Ozersk nuclear power plant, near the city of Chelyabinsk in Russia.

Justice denied

The British government requested the extradition of Lugovoy to face charges relating to Litvinenko's death. The request was denied. Kovtun was under investigation by the German authorities for suspected plutonium smuggling, but Germany dropped the case in 2009.

There can be little doubt why Litvinenko was killed. Two days after he died, representative Sergei Abeltsev told the Russian Duma: "The deserved punishment reached the traitor. I am confident that this terrible death will be a serious warning to traitors of all colours, wherever they are located. In Russia, they do not pardon treachery. I would recommend citizen Berezovsky to avoid any food at the commemoration for his accomplice Litvinenko."

After US security analyst Paul Joyal alleged that Litvinenko had been killed as a warning to all critics of the Putin government, he was shot outside his home in Maryland. Surviving several assassination attempts, Boris Berezovsky was then found dead in suspicious circumstances in his house at Sunninghill near Ascot in Berkshire on 23 March 2013. The verdict? Suicide.

As regards Litvinenko, Dmitry Kovtun and Andrei Lugovoy denied any wrongdoing, but a leaked US diplomatic cable revealed that Kovtun had left traces of radioactive polonium in the house and car he had used in Hamburg.

SALISBURY POISONING

In a case remarkably similar to that of Litvinenko, former Russian military intelligence officer and British spy Sergei Skripal and his daughter Yulia Skripal were poisoned in Salisbury, England, with a Novichok nerve agent on 4 March 2018. Developed in Russia, Novichok is thought to be one of the deadliest nerve agents ever produced.

Sergei Skripal at a court hearing in Russia in 2006, where he was convicted of high treason.

Sergei Skripal was an officer for Russia's Main Intelligence Directorate, the GRU, and worked as a double agent for Britain's Secret Intelligence Service from 1995 until his arrest in Moscow in December 2004. Convicted of high treason, he was sentenced to thirteen years in a penal colony in 2006. He was released and settled in England in 2010 after a spy swap. Yulia remained in Russia and was visiting her father. One theory was that the Russian secret services had somehow tricked her into carrying the deadly poison.

Britain maintained that the poisoning had been carried out by the Russian secret services and that was likely to have been ordered by Vladimir Putin himself. Sixty Russian diplomats were expelled from Britain. The Russians responded in kind. More than twenty other countries expelled Russian diplomats in support of the UK. Russia claimed that it had nothing to do with the poisoning and that Britain had the means and the motive to murder Skripal.

9/11: THE EVENTS OF 11 SEPTEMBER 2001

I n the wake of the US government's declaration of a "War on Terror" in 2001 came the questions and the theories. What happened on 11 September 2001 as terrorists crashed hijacked airliners into the

The dramatic scenes as Flight 175 is flown by the hijackers into the South Tower of the World Trade Center, some 20 minutes after the attack on the North Tower.

World Trade Center and the Pentagon? Did the US government actually carry out the attacks, to provide it with an excuse for an invasion of Iraq? Or was the Air Force's lack of reaction on that day simply due to poor intelligence and communication? Conspiracy theorists point to the unwillingness of the United States government to hold a full inquiry into the events of 11 September 2001. Dick Cheney initially opposed an investigation into the terrorist attacks. His reason was that resources and personnel would be taken away from the war on terrorism. It was over a year before the official investigation finally began. By contrast, the investigations into the attack on Pearl Harbor and the assassination of President Kennedy began after only nine and seven days respectively. When the 9/11 investigation finally got under way a number of inconsistent explanations were offered in response to questions relating to matters such as the failure of the military to prevent the attacks.

Perhaps the key to the prevalence of conspiracy theories is not so much the physical evidence as the belief that because of an ulterior motive the government condoned, or even positively encouraged, the terrible attacks. In the most popular of those theories, which was given a boost by the Michael Moore film *Fahrenheit 9/11*, it is reasoned that the United States government, dominated by powerful neo-conservatives and the oil business, welcomed the disaster in order to rally public support for a war in the Middle East. Although such a war would purport to be a war on terror it would really be a war for oil. It would also have the effect of increasing defence spending, which would be good for the government-linked defence industry. Finally it would also allow the passage of repressive new legislation, such as the USA Patriot Act which granted extra powers to the Federal Government. Seen from this conspiratorial point of view, the events of September 11 were basically a modern-day re-staging of the attack on Pearl Harbor or the sinking of the *Lusitania*, during which catastrophes (at least if you believe the conspiracy version) a government stood by and watched its own people massacred in order that it could drum up support for an unpopular war.

This is a scenario that persuaded many, particularly in the wake of the widely unpopular war in Iraq. But was it really credible? Did any of it really add up to proof that the United States government stood by and watched its citizens die?

Not according to *Popular Mechanics* magazine. This publication assembled a panel of experts and went through the theories relating to the destruction of the WTC twin towers. The findings of its experts suggested that some aspects of the collapse of the towers were unusual but not impossible – and, after all, how many times in the past have similar events taken place, thereby providing a comparison? In addition, the remainder of the "evidence" – the alleged

Smoke billows from the North Tower of the World Trade Center shortly after American Airlines Flight 11 crashed into it at 8.46 am local time.

cancellation of flights by Pentagon officials on the day of the attacks, for instance – was just as likely to be made up of a series of simple coincidences as anything more sinister. Also, the President's odd behaviour on hearing the news may simply have been a kind of panicked paralysis.

Overall, the suggestion that the government actively allowed the 9/11 attacks to take place is extremely far-fetched. The charge of incompetence is rather more likely to stick, of course, although the fact that enormous amounts of intelligence reach the United States government every day should be borne in mind.

On the other hand, it is hard to dismiss the allegation that the United States government and the oil and defence industries have done very well out of the War on Terror that followed the events of 11 September. This was one cloud whose lining had rather a lot of silver in it, especially if you were a Haliburton shareholder. As a result, the United States government may have been open to accusations that it has used the 9/11 tragedy to help its friends make profits – but that is quite a different thing from suborning mass murder. The conspiracy theorists may ultimately have a point, but to claim that the United States government masterminded the attacks is, in most people's view, stretching credibility more than a little far.

The WTC twin towers debate

The events of 11 September have produced what must be the most widely viewed news footage ever shot. On the face of it, you might think that there is no mystery at all about the events that have been so famously recorded. Arab terrorists hijacked four aircraft before flying two of them into the World Trade Center, another into the Pentagon and the fourth into a Pennsylvania field. Al-Qaeda claimed responsibility. Given that Al-Qaeda is not only a terrorist organization with a deep hatred of the United States but is also responsible for a previous attack on the World Trade Center, that is the end of the story, surely?

Well, not as far as the conspiracy theorists are concerned. They maintain that what we saw was a staged political stunt. And who was responsible? Why, the United States government of course. Depending on which version of the theory you subscribe to, the government either allowed a real Al-Qaeda attack to take place without preventing it or they carried out the whole operation themselves. So what possible evidence could there be for such an apparently outrageous supposition?p

Much of the more responsible conspiracy speculation focuses upon the lead-up to the attacks. The United States government was supplied with a considerable amount of intelligence that suggested that Al-Qaeda were planning an attack. While most of us might be inclined to put the government's lack of reaction down to incompetence, the more cynically minded see it as part of a deliberate pattern.

Let us begin by looking at the key events in detail, starting with the incident in which the two aircraft crashed into the twin towers of the WTC. To most observers, what happened seems simple enough: planes hit towers and explode, towers fall down. But it wasn't long before this version of the events became the subject of apparently well-informed speculation. The debate focused on whether or not the impact of the aircraft, coupled with the subsequent fire, would really be enough to bring down such huge structures.

What really brought down the twin towers?

According to some experts, buildings 1, 2, and 7 of the World Trade Center are the

The North Tower begins its spectacular collapse, accompanied by the mushroom cloud of concrete dust. This cloud has led many to conclude that explosives were used to collapse the tower.

only steel frame structures in history to have collapsed because of fire. Particularly controversial, because it had not been hit by an aircraft at all, is the fate of building number 7, which collapsed some hours after the two main towers. Furthermore, according to one demolition expert, the huge clouds of concrete dust that were seen billowing out of the towers were symptomatic of an explosion rather than a fire. Other alleged experts claim that the way in which the towers fell straight down had every appearance of controlled demolition. Finally, the wreckage from the towers appeared to contain molten steel. Fire would not cause steel to become molten – but a bomb would. The conspiracy theorists are clear about what these alleged facts add up to. They claim that the towers of the World Trade Center must have been rigged with explosives in order to make sure that the disaster was as dramatic as possible.

Then there is the Pentagon. The plane that crashed into the Pentagon was able to fly towards the building for forty minutes without being intercepted, despite the existence of sophisticated radar technology and anti-missile batteries – not to mention the building's proximity to Andrews Air Force Base. When the aircraft finally hit the building, it collided with the west wing, which was nearly empty at the time because of construction work. Once again, government complicity is the clear implication to the conspiracy theorists.

Perhaps the most famous piece in this particular conspiracy jigsaw is the notorious footage of President Bush reading a story to children in a kindergarten at the time that an aide announced that the first plane had struck the WTC. Instead of leaping into action the President simply carried on reading the story. In Michael Moore's film *Fahrenheit 9/11*, the footage was used to imply that Bush knew exactly what was going on. Further suspicious behaviour, in the eyes of the conspiracy theorists, came in the days following the attack. The government had neither produced the voice recorders nor the flight data recorders ("black boxes") from the aircraft that were involved in the New York attack. That had never happened in any previous

The Pentagon where it was struck by an airliner on 9/11. Critics of the official explanation claim that the original hole was too small to have been made by a 757.

major domestic crash. They have also failed to comment on whether or not the black boxes were recovered from the wreckage. There are also anomalies relating to the identity of the hijackers. Given the general level of carnage, much doubt has been cast on the discovery, near the Twin Towers, of an undamaged passport belonging to one of the hijackers. Furthermore, the identities of the nineteen hijackers are still much disputed. Waleed al-Shehri, one of the men named as being a hijacker by the FBI on their 9/11 attacks web page, later turned up alive and protested his innocence. The identities of three other hijackers were also in doubt.

Flight 93: the true story

The story of Flight 93, the fourth of the planes to be hijacked on 11 September, has become a modern legend. The passengers on Flight 93 were in a different situation to those in the other aircraft, who cannot have known that

the hijackers were planning to turn the planes into flying bombs. On Flight 93, however, thanks to the mobile phone, passengers were soon made all too aware of what was planned for them. Their plane was in the Washington region so it was more than likely that they were heading for the White House. If they just sat there and did nothing they were certain to die. Gradually, as we know from the final anguished phone calls to loved ones, the passengers decided to fight back. One of them, Todd Beamer, uttered the immortal words: "Let's roll".

And then there was silence. No more phone calls. The next thing anyone knows for certain is that Flight 93, a Boeing 757, crashed in rural Pennsylvania, near the town of Shanksville. The accepted story is that the passengers rose up and wrested control from the hijackers and that in the course of the struggle the plane went out of control and plunged into the ground. The passengers had sacrificed their lives in order that many more would be saved. They have been given the status of American heroes.

Today, there are not many who would dispute that the passengers were indeed heroes. However, there are plenty who wonder just exactly what caused the plane to plummet to the earth in such a way and who question the received version of events.

The final phone call
Essentially, the crash of Flight 93 is the subject of two alternative theories. The first of these maintains that there was an explosion on board the plane. This notion is given substance by the fact that in his final phone call a passenger said that one of the hijackers claimed to be carrying a bomb. The remaining option is that the aircraft was shot down on the orders of the United States government before it could hit its target. This is the theory that has aroused much controversy with its

suggestion that the government could have authorized the deaths of its own people.

So what evidence is there to suggest that such a thing might have happened? Well, first there is the timescale. By the time Flight 93 crashed everyone knew what had happened to the WTC twin towers and the Pentagon. A frantic search of United States airspace was taking place in order to establish whether or not any other planes had been hijacked. The United States government acknowledges that the first fighters with the mission to intercept took off at 8.52 a.m. and another set of fighters took off from Andrews Air Force Base near Washington at 9.35 a.m. – precisely the time that Flight 93 turned through almost 180 degrees and started heading straight for Washington. At that time, the F-16s were no more than ten minutes' flying time away, yet it was to be another thirty minutes before Flight 93 crashed. Surely one would have expected one of the F-16s to have reached the plane well before 10.06 a.m.?

To back up this line of thinking, there is evidence from a federal flight controller, published a few days later in New Hampshire. He said that an F-16 had been "in hot pursuit" of the hijacked United jet and "must have seen the whole thing". Also, immediately before the crash took place CBS television briefly reported that two F-16 fighters were tailing Flight 93. All fairly suspicious, but the question remains: would the United States government shoot its own plane down like that?

On 16 September Vice-President Dick Cheney announced that President Bush had authorized the Air Force pilots to shoot down hijacked commercial aircraft. This statement strongly supports the allegation that the F-16s that took off from Washington had been ordered to "protect the White House at all costs".

One might expect that the crash scene would offer a clear indication as to whether the aircraft was hit by a missile in the air or had simply hit the ground. This is where the controversy really starts to rage. Conspiracy theorists are convinced that the forensic evidence points to the plane having been brought down by a mid-air impact. The key evidence they cite is the wide dispersal of the aircraft's debris. Letters and other light refuse from the plane were discovered eight miles from the scene of the crash. The aircraft had disintegrated into pieces no more than two inches long and a section of one of the engines, which in itself weighed a ton, was found 600 yards from the site of the crash. Other remains of the plane were found two miles away near a town called Indian Lake. Furthermore, the debris was not scattered evenly along the route between the different sites but was grouped into distinct clusters. This, the conspiracy theorists argue, is clear evidence that debris was blown out of the plane by an initial mid-air explosion.

The mysterious white plane

The FBI, for its part, waved these suspicions away. The paper debris that was found eight miles away, they said, was blown there by the wind, while the engine section flew 600 yards due to the force of the aircraft's impact with the ground. They concluded that: "Nothing was found that was inconsistent with the plane going into the ground intact."

And if all this was not enough there is one final mystery that the conspiracy theorists point to: the mystery of the "white plane". Several eyewitnesses reported seeing a white plane flying very low just before Flight 93 crashed. At first the FBI denied that there had been any such plane in the neighbourhood. Then, as eyewitnesses continued to insist that they had seen such an aircraft, they announced that there had been a plane after all, a civilian business jet. Because it had been flying within twenty miles of Flight 93 the authorities had requested the pilot to descend from 37,000ft to 5,000ft in order to survey the crash site and transmit the map co-ordinates "for responding emergency crews". If anything, this explanation made the conspiracy theorists all the more suspicious. Firstly, by this time all non-military aircraft within the United States airspace had received clear orders to land at the nearest airport. Secondly, at a time of such uncertainty, and with F-16s supposedly in the vicinity, it seems utterly implausible that the military would seek assistance from the pilot of a civilian aircraft that just happened to be in the area.

So do the conspiracy theorists have a case? The evidence that F-16s *did* catch up with Flight 93 is certainly troubling, as is the pattern of the debris from the crash. And it is hard to believe that the government would have simply allowed the plane to come any closer to Washington. On the other hand, none of the witnesses to the aircraft's crash reported it as having been consumed by a fireball. If it was hit by a missile it certainly did not explode on impact. Perhaps consideration should be given to the less discussed possibility that one of the terrorists on board may have been carrying a bomb. It certainly ties all the elements of the story together: the heroic passengers take on the hijackers, then one of the hijackers accidentally or deliberately detonates the bomb, and the aircraft plunges to the ground before the pursuing F-16s are forced to confront the option of killing a plane-load of their fellow citizens. Whatever the full truth of the matter, what remains undeniable is the courage of the passengers who were caught up in this terrible situation.

THE OKLAHOMA CITY BOMBING

At the time that it was carried out – 19 April 1995 – the Oklahoma City bombing was the worst terrorist atrocity ever perpetrated on American soil. That grim record was comprehensively trumped six years later by the events of September 11, but at the time the Oklahoma bombing was a huge shock to the American system. What made it especially traumatic was the fact that it was not carried out by foreigners – Russians, Iraqis, or any other perceived enemies of America – but by Americans. Many Americans found this difficult to believe, which is perhaps why conspiracy theories very quickly grew up around the event. The suggestion was that it was the work of outsiders. Some of these theories can be dismissed, but there remain doubts about just exactly who was responsible for the bombing. Did Timothy McVeigh and his friends act entirely independently, as was argued at McVeigh's trial? Or was McVeigh simply a cog in a much bigger conspiracy that involved a whole gang of far-right activists?

The essential facts are not in question. In the early morning of 19 April 1995, Timothy McVeigh drove a rented yellow truck up to the Alfred P. Murrah Federal Building in Oklahoma City. He parked the truck in a parking space for the handicapped, just beneath an infant day-care centre. The truck was loaded with a huge and lethal fertilizer bomb, consisting of more than 6,000lbs of ammonium nitrate soaked in nitromethane fuel, plus an additional quantity of commercial Tovex explosive. The whole lot was wired up to blasting caps. At around 8.53 a.m., after he had parked the truck, McVeigh lit two fuses and walked quickly away, heading for his getaway car. He was wearing a T-shirt emblazoned with "Sic semper tyrannis", the words that were shouted by John Wilkes Booth as he assassinated Abraham Lincoln.

Timothy McVeigh in court. McVeigh managed to evade the forces of justice after the Oklahoma bombing for around three hours before being arrested for driving a car with no licence plate, possibly not an indication of a criminal mastermind.

Before McVeigh could reach the vehicle, he was knocked off his feet by the force of the explosion he had set off. Windows were smashed and buildings shook around him as he headed towards his getaway car, an 18-year-old Mercury Marquis. McVeigh got into the car and might well have made good his escape if it had not been for the fact that he was pulled over by a highway patrolman for not having a rear licence plate. When the patrolman checked the car, he found that McVeigh had a concealed firearm. The patrolman proceeded to take him into custody, little suspecting at this point that he had caught the man responsible for a bomb that had killed 168 people, injured 800 more, traumatized an entire city and shaken a nation.

Was there a second man?

Within 48 hours, though, the investigating officers had figured out that the guy with the missing licence plate was indeed the bomber they were looking for. At the time, however, that did not appear to be the end of the matter. The FBI were known to be looking for a second man, whom they believed to have been directly involved in the bombings. Gradually, though, this line of investigation seemed to peter out and when the case came to trial it was McVeigh alone who was accused of actually planting the bomb. He was duly convicted of murder and was sentenced to death, being executed by lethal injection at a US penitentiary in Terre Haute, Indiana, on 11 June 2001.

However, the question the conspiracy theorists wanted an answer to was – did McVeigh act alone or not? There is plenty of evidence to suggest that he did not. In the early stages of the investigation, the FBI were convinced that he had at least one

The Alfred P. Murrah Federal Building, Oklahoma City after it was bombed by ex-soldier with a grudge Timothy McVeigh on 19 April 1995. The attack was the worst terrorist outrage on US soil until 9/11.

partner in the operation. Numerous witnesses who saw McVeigh on the day of the bombing claim to have seen him with another man. They also claim to have seen a brown pick-up truck following the yellow Ryder truck. By some accounts, McVeigh and the second man were seen leaving the Murrah Building in the pick-up truck at just after 8 a.m., before returning in the yellow Ryder truck. At 8.45 a.m., the Ryder truck stopped at a convenience store and McVeigh was seen to buy two cokes and a packet of cigarettes, even though he was a non-smoker. Another eyewitness claimed to have seen McVeigh get into the Mercury along with another man. In all, at least ten different eyewitness statements suggested that there was at least one other person with McVeigh on the morning of the bombing.

All of that explains why the FBI spent the next year looking for a mystery second man, but it does not explain why, after a year's fruitless searching, they decided instead to promote the lone bomber theory in court. The idea that McVeigh did not act alone was given further credence when he was put through a polygraph test by his defence team. He passed on all questions concerning his own role but he failed when he denied that anybody else was involved.

It may well be that the FBI did not change their approach because of any sinister conspiracy but for the simple reason that they had a case against McVeigh and they were worried that the trial might collapse if the existence of an unknown second man was brought into the equation. It would have been easy for McVeigh to attempt to shift the responsibility on to this unknown man. If that was the case, the tactic was successful: McVeigh was found guilty. However, it did lead to unusual anomalies during the trial, such as the FBI's refusal to call any witnesses to McVeigh's movements (because they would all have mentioned that there was another man

with him). Privately, the FBI appear to have suspected that the second man died in the blast. There was one gruesome piece of evidence remaining after the bombing – a left leg whose owner had never been identified. Might the leg have belonged to the second man?

Whatever the case, no one identified the mystery man and the story that McVeigh was a lone bomber became the generally accepted truth.

Two of McVeigh's friends, Terry Nichols and Michael Fortier, were subsequently arrested. Both of them had sheltered McVeigh. Michael Fortier, who had sheltered and aided McVeigh before the bombing, but had then become a key FBI informant, was sentenced to twelve years in prison on 27 May 1998 on the charge of failing to warn the authorities about the attack.

The role played by Terry Nichols was harder to assess. At his federal trial, alongside McVeigh, he was sentenced to life imprisonment. In 2004 he was tried again, this time on state murder charges in Oklahoma, and was convicted of 160 counts of first-degree murder. The jury, however, were deadlocked on the question of whether or not this should result in a death sentence. As a result, the judge sentenced him to life without the possibility of parole.

Far-right militias

That should have been the end of the story. The FBI would certainly have been happy to have drawn a line under this terrible incident. However, it was hardly likely that the conspiracy aficionados would let things rest there. After all, there had been any number of rumours floating around from the very start. Some of the rumours came from those sympathetic to the far right. They were so accustomed to blaming the Federal Government for everything that they were not prepared to stop now. According to these obsessives, the Oklahoma bombing was actually carried out by the government

The empty chairs at the Oklahoma City Memorial represent the 168 people who died in the explosion.

in order to discredit the far right. There were unfounded allegations that federal employees had been warned not to go into work on the day of the bombing. Similar rumours circulated in the days following the events of 11 September.

Rather more plausible is the suggestion that the far-right militia movement was actually much more involved in the bombing than the FBI were prepared to admit. Following McVeigh's confession and his subsequent conviction, this was the direction in which most conspiracy theorists started to look. In particular, some assiduous reporters began to find clear links between McVeigh and a gang of far-right militia men that was connected to the Aryan Republican Army. The gang, led by Peter Langan and Richard Guthrie, carried out a series of bank robberies across the Midwest during the mid-1990s.

Close investigation revealed that McVeigh had been in the same place at the same time as the gang over the years. During those periods, he was able to travel continually and he always had money without having a job. He also told friends about a group that he had become involved with. For years, rumours of McVeigh's connection with the gang circulated but for a long time the FBI refused to accept the link.

All that changed when, early in 2004, Associated Press revealed that blasting caps of the type used in Oklahoma City had been found at the gang's compound when they were arrested in 1996. Furthermore, the gang were in possession of a driving licence that belonged to a gun dealer who had been robbed by McVeigh immediately before the bombing. These revelations were deeply embarrassing to the FBI and they resulted in an internal inquiry being launched into the matter in March 2004. As yet, however, no conclusions from this inquiry have been made public.

A cover-up?

So was there a wider conspiracy or did McVeigh act alone? In this case, it definitely looks as if the conspiracy theorists have a point. The evidence of links between McVeigh and the Midwest bank robbers is extremely persuasive, especially when it is backed up by the fact that so many eyewitnesses recalled seeing McVeigh with other men on the day of the bombing. And the reasons for the cover-up? Probably simple incompetence and the desire to make sure that there was a successful outcome at the trial – one that would make a nice neat story and reassure the American people that justice had been done. Unfortunately, the result of this apparent deceit was to further entrench the mistrust of government in the minds of many Americans and make them all the more likely to give credit to outlandish conspiracy theories – like those, indeed, that McVeigh and his cohorts believed in.

CHAPTER TWO:
SECRET SOCIETIES

Throughout history, men – and women, but it is predominantly men – have formed societies for the mutual advancement of their members, to share one another's proclivities, or simply to socialize with like-minded individuals. That some of these societies have been secretive, cannot be denied. But just how suspicious should we be of these mysterious groups of people?

THE BILDERBERG GROUP

All Bilderberg meetings take place in impressive settings amidst tight security, such as this one in Dresden in 2009.

It may well be the oldest conspiracy theory of all – that the world is controlled by a shadowy cabal of powerful men and women. Often, the existence of such groups is dubious in the extreme – as with, for instance, the Illuminati. In other cases, there may be some basis in fact (for example, it is true that there are many powerful Jewish bankers) but the leap to conspiracy (that Jewish bankers are running the world) is nothing more than the product of a delusion, in this case a form of anti-Semitic paranoia.

However, the Bilderberg Group does at least look as if it might just be the genuine article – a group whose members rule the world. To begin with, it is clear that the Bilderberg Group does actually exist. It was founded over sixty years ago and it has held an annual meeting ever since. And it is undoubtedly a secret organization. It has no corporate presence, not even a website, and it goes to some lengths to keep its annual meeting place – which is different each year – a secret. Finally, it does indeed involve many of the most powerful men, and women, in the world. Henry Kissinger and Paul Wolfowitz are regular attendees as are numerous Rockefellers, Fords, and Agnellis. Even more significant, as far as the conspiracy theorists are concerned, is the fact that Margaret Thatcher, Bill Clinton, and Tony Blair all attended before they came to lead their countries. Coincidence, or something more sinister?

Secret meetings

So what are the known facts about this mysterious organization? It was founded in 1954 and it took its name from the hotel in the Netherlands where the first meeting was held. Its founder members were British politician Denis Healey, Joseph Retinger, David Rockefeller, and Prince Bernhard of the Netherlands, a man who, it is often pointed out, was a member of the Nazi party in his youth (though how that impacts upon those conspiracy theorists who see the Bilderberg Group as a Jewish conspiracy is anyone's guess).

The group is still based in the Netherlands, for administrative purposes at least. It maintains an office in the quiet town of Leiden. Phone calls to the office, however, are invariably met with an anonymous answerphone message.

The official purpose of the Bilderberg group, inasmuch as it has been publicly expressed, was to further the understanding between Western Europe and North America through informal meetings between powerful individuals. If it had an agenda, as founder member Lord Healey used to say, it was to promote democracy across the globe. To this end, a steering committee draws up an invitation list each year with up to a hundred names on it, all of them either European or North American. The location of the annual meeting is fixed, with countries taking it in turns to host the meetings. Funding for

the conferences is then raised from friendly corporations like Nokia or Fiat, for these conferences are where the top names in politics and industry meet. The list of participants is made available to the public, but the topics of the discussions are not. And attendees have to promise not to reveal what has been said at Bilderberg meetings. This secrecy, of course, has attracted much coverage and has provided the conspiracy theorists with ammunition. Bilderbergers themselves claim that it is not secrecy but privacy – and that privacy is essential if prominent people are to be allowed to speak freely, without the fear of media attention.

A darker purpose?

One thing is for sure, though. Few people ever turn down an invitation to a Bilderberg event and attending one of their meetings is almost always a good career move. Some say that this is just the way of the world. There are plenty of exclusive clubs where the rich and powerful meet away from prying eyes: the Bilderberg is simply the most exclusive club of them all.

Its members like to suggest that the Bilderberg Group is a benign organization, a think-tank dedicated to the values of liberal democracy, whose interest is simply in helping the world to run better. Its critics, however, feel that the group has a much darker purpose. They find it hard to believe that an organization that is genuinely committed to democracy should feel the need to shroud its discussions in secrecy. At best, say the critics, the Bilderberg is an engine of globalization, an organization dedicated to producing a bland new world where we all consume the same goods, watch the same TV shows, and believe the same identikit politicians. A world, in short, that is run for profit. Earth plc.

Others feel that the aims of the group are more sinister yet. They claim that the Bilderberg is an actively neo-Nazi organization that is working to build a world fascist state. Others suggest that the Bilderberg Group is simply the latest front organization for the Illuminati, the secret rulers of the world for centuries.

So which of these is the Bilderberg? Benign talking shop or sinister cabal? There seems to be little or no evidence for the more extreme claims. However, the accusation that this is an organization that is committed to globalization seems to have some substance. It is surely no coincidence that one of the delegates in 2005 was Mrs Bill Gates, wife of the supreme globalizer. Yet globalization is hardly a secret matter: one has only to walk down any shopping street from Berlin to Baltimore to see that. Perhaps the truth of the matter is that today, political, media, and commercial power is increasingly concentrated in an ever-smaller number of hands, and that the Bilderberg Group is part of that process. It is not so much a shadowy organization of world rulers but an informal group of people whose economic power already dominates our lives, whose brand names are written on almost everything we consume and who wish to further their global interests. And that, of course, is no secret.

Ex-US Secretary of State Henry Kissinger, former Vice President Nelson Rockefeller, and former President Gerald Ford in the White House. Henry Kissinger is one of many high-profile members of the Bilderberg Group.

THE ILLUMINATI

The Illuminati are one of the great touchstones of conspiracy theory. This is the shadowy group that the conspiracy theorists believe are behind practically everything that takes place in the world – capitalism or communism, Zionism or Catholicism. The British royal family, the American presidency, Freemasons, the Knights Templar, even extra-terrestrials – all of them are bound up with the Illuminati, the secret rulers of the world. And of course the fact that there is no evidence of the existence of the Illuminati is actually proof of their all-powerful nature, rather than of their non-existence.

So who are – or were – the Illuminati and why are they credited with such extraordinary powers? The first part of this question is easy enough to answer. The Illuminati were a group founded in Bavaria, Germany, in the late eighteenth century by an ex-Jesuit named Adam Weishaupt, a professor of canon law in Ingolstadt, Germany. Much taken with the ideas of the Enlightenment, he decided to form a group of fellow republican freethinkers which would be clandestine, because it was dangerous to hold such ideas at that time. Together with one Baron Adolph von Knigge, he founded his movement on 1 May 1776, calling it the "Perfectibilists". However, its adherents soon became known as the Illuminati. They were also sometimes referred to as the Illuminati Order, the Order of the Illuminati or the Bavarian Illuminati.

Many of those attracted to the new movement were already Freemasons, which accounts for the perceived links between the two, quite different, movements. Members had

Adam Weishaupt, the eighteenth-century political and religious radical who founded the society known as the Illuminati.

to pledge obedience to their superiors and were divided into three classes. The first class was called the Nursery, and it included the offices of Preparation, Novice, Minerval, and Illuminatus Minor; the second was known as the Masonry and it embraced the higher ranks of Illuminatus Major and Illuminatus Dirigens; and the third class was referred to as the Mysteries and within it were the Lesser Mysteries, the ranks of Presbyter and Regent and the Greater Mysteries, the highest ranks of Magus and Rex.

The Illuminati managed to start branches in most European countries in the first few years of its existence, with many influential intellectuals and progressive politicians counting themselves as members – among them such luminaries as the great German writer Goethe and the dukes of Gotha and Weimar. The total membership of the group at this point has been estimated at 2,000.

However, the association's radical ideas soon attracted the dislike of the powerful Catholic Church which, in 1784, persuaded the Bavarian government to pass a law banning all secret societies, including the Illuminati and the Freemasons. According to all the official accounts this resulted in the disappearance of the Illuminati. The order was already suffering from internal schisms and it was finally wound up in 1790.

A single world government

No sooner had the Illuminati come to an official end than the conspiracy theories began. Just seven years later, in 1797, a French cleric called Abbé Augustin Barruél published a book called *Memoirs Illustrating the History of Jacobinism*, in which he set out a conspiracy theory involving the Illuminati, along with the Knights Templar, the Rosicrucians and, as his book title suggests, the Jacobins. In the following year a Scottish professor of natural history named John Robison published the first part of a book with the unwieldy title of *Proofs of a Conspiracy Against all the Religions and Governments of Europe, Carried on in the Secret Meetings of Free Masons, Illuminati, and Reading Societies, Collected from Good Authorities*. Robison's thesis was that an Illuminati conspiracy was planning to replace all religions with humanism and nation states with a single world government.

This linking of the Illuminati with Freemasonry and the further linking of the combined institutions with the sinister

Thomas Jefferson, US president from 1801 to 1809: sympathizer or member of the Illuminati?

manipulation of society began to gain credence. However, not everyone was convinced. No less a person than Thomas Jefferson declared that he could quite understand why the Illuminati had been driven to secrecy:

> As Weishaupt lived under the tyranny of a despot and priests, he knew that caution was necessary even in spreading information, and the principles of pure morality... If Weishaupt had written here, where no secrecy is necessary in our endeavours to render men wise and virtuous, he would not have thought of any secret machinery for that purpose.

Of course, the conspiracy theorists saw this as proof that Jefferson himself was one of the Illuminati. And, indeed, it was not long before rumours of Illuminati involvement in American affairs began to circulate. The symbol of the all-seeing pyramid in the Great Seal of the United States was cited as a secret sign, painted by high-ranking members of the Illuminati whose intention was to show how the Illuminati's ever-present watchful eye surveyed the Americans.

It has also been suggested that the Yale-based secret society Skull and Bones was founded as the American branch of the Illuminati.

In recent times, conspiracy theories involving the Illuminati have become ever more bizarre. Books and internet sites explain that the Illuminati are responsible for almost everything, whether it be the assassination of President Kennedy or the foundation of the Jehovah's Witnesses. The fact that there is no evidence of the group is always presented as conclusive proof of its secret existence.

Extra-terrestrial reptiles

Perhaps the most extraordinary of all the Illuminati-linked theories is that put forward by a former British soccer player and sports commentator named David Icke. According to Icke the Illuminati are indeed the secret rulers of the world but they date back a lot further than the Bavaria of the 1780s. In fact, says Icke, the Illuminati are reptilian extra-terrestrials who have controlled the world for thousands of years, and have been operating from the fourth dimension (which explains why we have not noticed them yet).

While Icke's theory has not attracted a huge following, there are still many who believe that the Illuminati – while not reptilian aliens – do exist. And it may well be true that the world's powerful people do talk discreetly to each other within secret organizations. However, the suggestion that they are linked by membership of the Illuminati, a quasi-Masonic group that is devoted to republican freethinking, seems more than a little unlikely. Or is that just what our reptilian overlords want us to believe...?

One-time goalkeeper and sports presenter David Icke, now a conspiracy theorist of the first order, and scourge of reptilian aliens wherever they may be hiding.

SECRETS OF THE CATHOLIC CHURCH

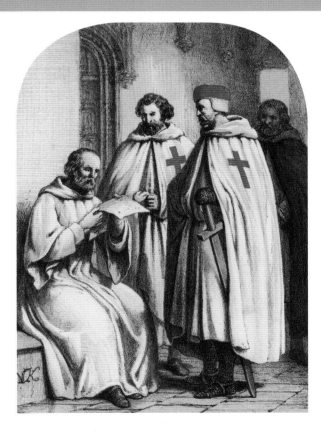

Members of the military order of the Templars. The order was persecuted for heresy and then disbanded by the French King Philip IV in 1307, but the conspiracy theories surrounding it have not gone away.

The Christian Church has been a natural target for conspiracy theorists throughout almost the whole of its existence. In centuries past, these theorists would have been called heretics and burnt at the stake. In these more enlightened days they post their ideas on the internet and write bestselling novels.

The Knights Templar and the Holy Grail

Two subjects that appeal to conspiracy theorists are the Knights Templar and the Holy Grail. The Knights Templar were an order of warrior monks based in Jerusalem during the time of the Crusades. They were believed to be fabulously wealthy and they became so powerful that in 1307 Philip IV of France led a campaign against them. Members of the order were arrested and tortured until they confessed to heresy. Their influence lingered on for many years, especially in Portugal and Scotland, but they gradually disappeared from view. However, many theorists believe that the order actually went underground instead of dying out and that it is still in existence.

Even more mysterious than the Knights Templar is the Holy Grail, one of the great myths of Christianity. The Holy Grail was supposedly the cup that caught the blood of Jesus during his crucifixion. The story goes that the cup was kept by a friend of Jesus, Joseph of Arimathea, who might have taken it to France, or perhaps even Glastonbury in England. Some believe that it was taken to Jerusalem in the Holy Land: others claim that it has been kept in Genoa, Valencia, or Rosslyn Chapel in Scotland. According to some accounts, it might even have fallen into the hands of the Knights Templar. Wherever it landed up, it became a mythical object over time and it was credited with extraordinary magical powers.

The mystical Holy Grail, sought after for centuries but perhaps just a metaphor for the bloodline of Jesus.

Stories have circulated about the Holy Grail and the Knights Templar for centuries, but a modern bestseller *Holy Blood, Holy Grail*, published in 1982, suggested that behind these mysteries lay an even greater one – one that went to the very heart of the Christian faith. According to the authors of the book, the Holy Grail was not a cup at all: that was the result of a mistake in translation. The real Christian treasure was not the Holy Grail but the Holy Blood. That is, the true secret was not the existence of a mere cup but of a bloodline of the descendants of Jesus.

The Magdalene conspiracy

According to this theory, Jesus had two children, the products of a clandestine marriage to Mary Magdalene. These children, so the story goes, were brought to France by Mary Magdalene and Joseph of Arimathea. The oldest child died but the second son went on to have children whose descendants would become the (real) Merovingian Kings of France between the fifth and eighth centuries AD. After the Merovingian Kings were overthrown, their legacy was protected by the Knights Templar and their great secret – together with the evidence to back it up – was hidden away. Its existence was only hinted at by obscure codes.

With the end of the Knights Templar, so this theory goes, all evidence of the bloodline of Jesus disappeared from view for over 500 years. It was only in 1885 that someone began to penetrate the mystery, a young priest named François Bérenger Saunière, who was assigned to the parish at Rennes-le-Chateau, an ancient walled town in the French Pyrenees.

Saunière began to restore the town's sixth-century church. As he did so, he found a series of parchments hidden inside a hollow pillar. These parchments included some genealogical information and a collection of ciphers and

The risen Christ appears to Mary Magdalene in Veronese's painting Noli Me Tangere. *But was Christ ever actually dead?*

codes. Allegedly the secrets of these codes made Saunière a wealthy man and he later spent much of his money on commissioning strange new artefacts for the church.

The Priory of Sion

With Saunière's death the trail once again went cold, only to be revived by a Frenchman named Pierre Plantard who wrote extensively about the mysteries of Rennes-le-Chateau. He claimed that knowledge of the descendants of Jesus had remained in the hands of a mysterious organization called the Priory of Sion, an ancient secret order that lay behind the Knights Templar and guarded their legacy. Notable members included Leonardo da Vinci and Isaac Newton.

Sadly, this exotic theory did not convince many historians, many of whom were amused to discover that Pierre Plantard had registered the Priory of Sion as his own organization. He had also transparently forged genealogical documents, allegedly discovered by Saunière, which appeared to demonstrate that Plantard himself was a direct descendant of the Merovingian Kings – and thus of Jesus Christ himself!

And if all that sounds like the stuff of best-selling fiction rather than history, author Dan Brown can only agree with you. This most entertaining but unlikely of conspiracy theories formed the basis of his global bestseller, *The Da Vinci Code*.

GOD'S BANKER: THE DEATH OF ROBERTO CALVI

Roberto Calvi in a Milan Courtroom 1981, after spending three years on the run. Calvi was sentenced to four years in prison for fraud, but was released on bail to await an appeal.

The death of Roberto Calvi, nicknamed "God's banker" because of his close links with the Vatican, shocked the world in 1982, when he was found hanging beneath Blackfriars Bridge in London. Initially, his death was seen as suicide, but it soon emerged that murder was a much more likely scenario. Disturbing evidence came to light when the case was investigated, for it appeared that Calvi's shady financial dealings not only involved Italy's largest private bank and a secret Italian Masonic organization but the Vatican itself. To this day, the complex plot involving the bank, the Freemasons, and the Vatican continues to unravel and it is still unclear exactly what happened. However, there seems to be no doubt that the Vatican was politically and financially implicated in the scandal, whether directly or indirectly.

Shady dealings

At the time of his death, 62-year-old Calvi was a successful businessman, the chairman of Banco Ambrosiana in Milan. Over his career he had built the bank up from a small concern to a large international organization with a huge financial empire. However, in 1978 Banco Ambrosiana was investigated by the Bank of Italy and found to be guilty of illegally exporting billions of lire. Calvi went on the run, and the bank began to collapse. Three years later, he was arrested, tried and sentenced to four years in prison. After a short period of detention he was released on bail pending an appeal, but he had other charges to answer as well. At the time of his murder he was also being investigated for making fraudulent deals in the United States with a Sicilian banker called Michele Sindona.

As the investigations continued it emerged that the Vatican had a shareholding in Banco Ambrosiana and that Calvi was closely linked to Archbishop Paul Marcinkus, the head of the Vatican Bank. Enormous sums of money had been siphoned off from Banco Ambrosiana into the so-called "Institute for Religious Works", headed by Marcinkus, and there was speculation that this money had gone to fund right-wing regimes in Latin America that were friendly to the United States government and the Vatican. Another player in this complex game was Licio Gelli, a former Nazi, who ran a Masonic lodge known as Propaganda Due, or P2. This secret organization had a membership of over 1,000 prominent politicians, businessmen, and criminals, who were all united in a spirit of anti-

communism as well as being dedicated to the enhancement of their own personal wealth and power.

Murder not suicide

In 1998 Calvi's family caused his body to be exhumed and, four years later, the initial verdict of suicide was overturned. It transpired that Calvi had been found with five bricks in his pocket and his hands tied behind his back. Moreover, his neck showed no signs of damage and there were none of his own fingerprints on the bricks. All of this pointed to the fact that he had not committed suicide as a reaction to financial ruination, but had been cold-bloodedly murdered by his enemies in the world of high finance and organized crime.

The killing had all the hallmarks of a Mafia-style execution. Police in Rome and London began to track down several suspects. Pippo Calo, a prominent member of the Sicilian Mafia; Flavio Carboni, a businessman with many interests all over the world; Carboni's ex-girlfriend, Manuela Kleinzig; Ernesto Diotallevi, the leader of a criminal organization in Rome called the "Banda della Magliana"; and a Mafia financier named Francesco Di Carlo. On 18 April 2005, the City of London police force charged Calo, Carboni, Kleinzig, and Diotallevi with the murder.

An unholy mob

In recent years, it has been suggested that the real reason that Calvi was murdered was to prevent him from making known the links between the Vatican, the P2 Freemasons, and the Mafia. During his time at Banco Ambrosiana, enormous sums of money were transferred into the Vatican's coffers, resulting in the ultimate bankruptcy of Ambrosiana and its shareholders. (The day before Calvi died, his secretary Teresa Corrocher committed suicide by jumping out of a high window at the bank's headquarters. She left a note blaming her boss.)

It seems that Calvi and Gelli were in league. Calvi had been passing money from Ambrosiano and the Vatican Bank to Gelli and others, who in turn were busy negotiating political deals such as the sale of the Exocet missile from France to Argentina. In the view of many critics, the Vatican acted as a country with right-wing political interests, bankrolling whatever initiatives seemed beneficial to the Pope and the Catholic church, whether in Latin America or Europe. This was done secretly, with no regard whatsoever to democratic or sovereign rights in those countries. Obviously, if any of this information came out, it would be highly damaging to the Pope and the Vatican, who liked to preserve an image of being above politics.

The death of John Paul I

When John Paul I took office as Pope in 1978, it looked as though some of the activities of Archbishop Marcinkus and the "Institute for Religious Works" would have to come to an end. However, John Paul I died only thirty-three days after his election, apparently of a heart attack. Some suspected foul play and

indeed there were a number of anomalies surrounding the death, which was not well handled by the Vatican health carers. The Vatican press office also made many errors in reporting the death. In keeping with Vatican law, no post-mortem was performed on the Pope, which also caused some commentators to question what had happened. A controversy ensued, with some claiming that the Pope had been murdered and others holding the opposite view. For example, in his book, *In God's Name*, David Yallop suggested that the Pope had been in danger the moment he took office. John Cornwell rejected this theory in his own book, *A Thief in the Night,* claiming that the Pope died as the result of a pulmonary embolism. He further suggested that the Vatican had acted in an incompetent, rather than a criminal, manner both during and after the tragedy. Whatever the truth of the matter, it seems that in terms of its political and financial dealings in the 1970s and 1980s, the Vatican had a great deal to hide. To this day, we still do not know the full extent of its involvement in the Calvi affair. Perhaps the ongoing trial will finally reveal the truth.

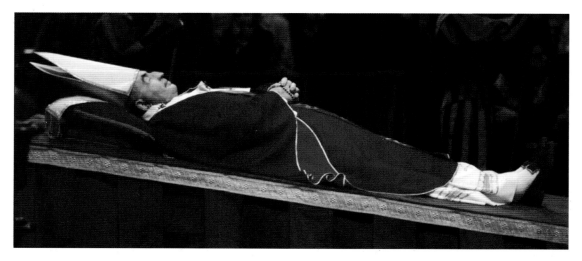

John Paul I lying in state after he passed away in 1979, just 33 days after becoming Pope.

THE PROTOCOLS OF THE ELDERS OF ZION

Vladimir Lenin preaches to the masses, Russia 1917. The fact that some Bolshevik leaders were Jewish was taken by many as proof of the worldwide Jewish conspiracy.

The document known as *The Protocols of the Elders of Zion* is one of the earliest, most successful and enduring of all conspiracy theories. First circulated in Russia during the early twentieth century it purports to be a kind of manual for world domination that was written by a mysterious cabal of Jewish elders. It was then used to fuel fears that there was an international Jewish conspiracy that sought to take over the world. So successful was it in its aims that it has been used again and again over the ensuing century. Wherever there has been a rush of anti-Semitism, from Hitler's Germany to the training camps of Al-Qaeda, you can guarantee that a copy of *The Protocols of the Elders of Zion* will never be hard to find.

The document may only have appeared in its currently recognized form in the final years of Tsarist Russia, but it has its roots in the mid-nineteenth century. The story begins with a French popular novel called *The Mysteries of the People*, written by Eugène Sue, which featured a group of Jesuits that were plotting to take over the world. This notion of a massive conspiracy was then taken up by the French satirist Maurice Joly, who used it in an 1864 pamphlet titled

"Dialogues in Hell Between Machiavelli and Montesquieu", a document which attacked the political ambitions of the then French ruler, Napoleon III. This time, however, the plotters, as the title suggests, were operating from beyond the grave.

Then, in 1868, Hermann Goedsche, a German anti-Semite and spy, wrote a book named *Biarritz*. This included a chapter entitled "The Jewish Cemetery in Prague and the Council of Representatives of the Twelve Tribes of Israel". The chapter described an imaginary secret rabbinical cabal meeting which was held in the cemetery at midnight every hundred years to plan the agenda for the Jewish Conspiracy. The set-up was plainly taken from an Alexandre Dumas novel, while the supposed secret agenda was actually straight from Joly's "Dialogues in Hell...".

Secret police

However, turning the supposed conspirators from Jesuits or dead philosophers into Jews touched a nerve and by the 1890s copies of this chapter of Goedsche's book, now treated as fact rather than fantasy or satire, were starting to circulate in Russia. Before long the Tsar's secret police, the Okhrana, recognized the potential popularity of the material and one of their operatives, Matvei Golovinski, worked up a book-length version of this fantastical Zionist plot. The book, now known as *The Protocols of the Elders of Zion,* was widely circulated and was undoubtedly influential in inflaming the anti-Jewish pogrom that swept Russia in 1905–1906.

Curiously, one of the visions put forward by the *Protocols* – that of a small group taking over a huge country – was repeated by the real events of a decade later when the 1917 Bolshevik Revolution transformed Russia. Before long this was seen by many as evidence that the Bolshevik revolution was in fact part of the Jewish conspiracy. Jews and communists were now bracketed together across much of the world and the *Protocols* were put forward as damning evidence.

The *Protocols* were popular with right wing elements in 1920s Germany and also in the United States. No less a man than Henry Ford sponsored the printing of half a million copies in America.

Then the debunking began in earnest. Experts looked at the document and soon noticed that its origins lay in pulp fiction rather than historical fact. In 1920, one Lucien Wolf published an exposé tracing the history of the Protocols back to the works of Goedsche and Joly. The *Times* soon followed suit and, later that year, a book documenting the hoax was published in the United States by Herman Bernstein.

Adolf Hitler

One might have thought that this would have been the end of the tale. Sadly not. By the 1920s anti-Semitism was endemic, nowhere more so than in Germany. Adolf Hitler referred to the *Protocols* in *Mein Kampf*: "To what extent the whole existence of this people is based on a continuous lie is shown incomparably by the *Protocols of the Wise Men of Zion*, so infinitely hated by the Jews", he wrote. He acknowledged the claims that the book was a forgery but ignored them, claiming instead that "with positively terrifying certainty they reveal the nature and activity of the Jewish

Senior members of the Nazi Party, including Adolf Hitler (second left), Rudolf Hess (second right), and Julius Streicher (right), circa 1937.

people and expose their inner contexts as well as their ultimate final aims."

Once the Nazis took power in Germany the book became a set text in schools and helped fuel all the horrors of the Holocaust. It did not matter to the German Nazis that in 1934 a Swiss Nazi was brought to court after he had published a series of articles accepting the *Protocols* as fact. The trial, known as the Berne Trial, finished in May 1935 when the court declared the *Protocols* to be forgeries, plagiarisms, and obscene literature. As far as Hitler was concerned, however, a lurid lie beat the truth every time and the Swiss verdict was completely ignored.

The palpable falsity of the *Protocols* has not stopped their circulation in more recent times, either. They are widely published across the Arab world and have proved particularly popular in Iran, Egypt, and Saudi Arabia, where they have been used to inflame opinion over the whole Palestinian question. In America, too, the Protocols are still accepted as fact by both neo-Nazi organizations and Louis Farrakhan's Nation of Islam, which has distributed copies.

The history of the *Protocols* demonstrates that a powerful conspiracy theory need not have any factual basis to gain acceptance: it also reminds us that false conspiracy theories can do an enormous amount of harm if they are cynically used to back up the worst political objectives and to persecute innocent people.

CHAPTER THREE:
THE UNKNOWN

Although nineteenth-century authors such as Jules Verne speculated on the subject of alien life-forms, it was not until the second half of the twentieth century that the existence of beings from other worlds became such a passionately held conviction. The questions remain: do such life-forms exist, have they travelled millions of light years to visit us, and are governments of the world in collusion to cover up these visits?

FLYING SAUCERS: THE ROSWELL INCIDENT

Aliens and their spaceship on display at the International UFO Museum and Research Center in Roswell, New Mexico.

The Roswell Incident of June 1947 remains one of the most intriguing episodes in the history of UFO research. For many, it is the most persuasive evidence we have that alien beings exist, that they travel about the cosmos in spacecraft and that they once landed here on Earth.

The story began in 1947 when a pilot named Kenneth Arnold claimed that he had seen several objects flying "like geese" through the sky near Mount Rainier, Washington. He described them "moving like a saucer would if it skimmed across the water". The journalist reporting the story coined the term "flying saucer" to describe the craft and this has been used informally

ever since to denote UFOs – unidentified flying objects.

Whether such objects exist, and whether Arnold was telling the truth when he made the claim that day, has been the subject of much speculation over the years. For what happened a few weeks afterwards confirmed, in many people's minds, that aliens had indeed visited our planet and that the American government, for reasons of its own, tried to hush up the story.

Extra-terrestrial crash landing?

In early July 1947, a rancher named William "Mack" Brazel was riding out over land near Corona, New Mexico when he noticed a large amount of strange-looking debris scattered

The story that launched a thousand saucers: the Daily Record *of 8 July 1947 reports the Roswell "incident".*

about. He informed Sheriff Wilcox of Chaves County who, thinking this must be to do with military exercises, passed the information on to the Army Air Force base at Roswell. Major Jesse Marcel, the base intelligence officer, was instructed to examine the debris. Meanwhile, a local newspaper published the story, reporting that a "flying saucer" had landed on the ranch (they also claimed that it had "been captured", which was a complete fabrication). The matter was then referred to the United States Army Air Force research laboratories, who issued a statement to the effect that the debris was not a flying saucer but the remains of a high altitude weather balloon with a radar attachment made of aluminium and balsa wood, that was being used for State purposes.

After the sighting in New Mexico, the press picked up the story and many newspapers across the United States published more or less lurid accounts of it. Public interest ran high and various other sightings were reported during the summer of 1947. However, the Army's insistence that the wreckage was not a crashed or captured flying saucer but simply the remains of a weather balloon eventually began to quell press and public interest in the subject.

The evidence

The Roswell Incident, as it came to be called, looked destined to slip into obscurity for many years, but in 1978 a UFO researcher named Stanton Friedman began to delve into it once again. While on a lecture tour, he received a call from Jesse Marcel, who had handled the affair back in 1947. However, Marcel could not remember the date on which the incident took place. With the help of co-researcher William Moore, Friedman began to find out more and eventually unearthed newspaper clippings reporting the story. Then the pair began to ask questions. What kind of weather balloon could yield such strange debris? Brazel and others had said that the material they had found was extremely light and could not be burned or otherwise destroyed. Why would they lie about such a thing? And why was the whole affair cloaked in such secrecy? The Army seemed to have something to hide – what was it?

Little green men

Friedman and Moore interviewed a teletype operator named Lydia Sleppy. She had worked at a New Mexico radio station in 1947 and had claimed that the FBI had interrupted the transmission of the "flying saucer" story. This seemed to tally with Marcel's account, in which he had stated that the army had suppressed information about the strange debris that he had seen with his own eyes and that the "weather balloon" story had been a cover up. A retired Air Force brigadier general called Arthur Exon then came out of the woodwork. He told UFO researchers Kevin Randle and Donald Schmitt that some strange debris had been brought in while he had

Area 51 is still a restricted site, a fact pointed out by conspiracy theorists who believe the government has something to hide.

been working at the Wright Patterson Air Force Base in 1947. It was lightweight and apparently indestructible. There were also rumours circulating around the base, he said, that bodies had been recovered out of a "craft from space".

Another retired Air Force officer, Brigadier General Thomas Dubose, alleged in interviews that the Roswell Incident had been treated with the greatest secrecy and that the White House had been involved. He also confirmed that the "weather balloon" story had been fabricated. Other senior ex-officers then emerged with similar tales to tell: they had either seen the bodies of alien creatures who had died when the craft crashed or they had heard of their existence.

Much of this evidence was dismissed by sceptics as second-hand. Yet there remained disturbing anomalies in the government's weather balloon story, so – not surprisingly – questions continued to be asked.

Secret surveillance?

Several theories were advanced. The first, and in the opinion of many people, the most persuasive, was that the debris was surveillance equipment that was being used in a top secret government project designed to spy on Russian nuclear activity, called Mogul. The incident needed to be hushed up because of the clandestine nature of the operation, which is why the army came up with the story about the weather balloon. However, this theory does not explain why the material found on the ranch was so unusual, or why the army would be using such material. It was also pointed out that the army had previously been unconcerned about people stumbling across the evidence of balloons and other army equipment found scattered in the desert: but this time they rushed to hide it.

Next came the idea that the incident could be attributed to a nuclear accident on the part of the army but, once again, there were problems with this explanation. For a start, the army had no assembled nuclear weapons in its arsenal at the time and there were no other nuclear accidents during the period in question, as public records now attest. Critics also argued that if the army had lost a nuclear weapon in the desert they would surely not have waited for a passing rancher to let them know where it was!

So what really happened?

Because of the government's secrecy surrounding the issue, a number of UFO researchers have come to the conclusion that some kind of covert activity must have taken place. Some believe that there was an alien landing and that the United States government simply denied the fact in order to prevent panic among the public. Others suggest that the government has access to alien technology but refuses to admit it. There has even been speculation that this was either a crash between two alien spacecraft or a crash involving a spy craft which secretly experimented on live human beings. This latter theory, advanced by Nick Redfern in his book *Body Snatchers in the Desert*, has gained credibility within the UFO field, if not outside it.

Ultimately, it seems that right up to this day nobody really knows what took place. Even the most persuasive theories that have been advanced appear to be full of loose ends. However, whether or not we believe that alien beings landed in the desert that day, what we do know is that there was a lot more to the incident than a burst weather balloon. And that is why, for the foreseeable future, UFO researchers and others will continue to ask: what really happened at Roswell?

THE RENDLESHAM AFFAIR

I n the early hours of Boxing Day, 1980, a strange incident occurred in Rendlesham Forest, Suffolk. Close to the pine forest was an American Air Force Base, which suddenly began to track an unidentified craft on its radar. The base was immediately put on full alert, but after a while it became clear that the craft was not aggressive and that there was no real threat. However, a patrol was sent to the forest to investigate. After the patrol had reached the site by following a dark, narrow path the men saw bright beams of red and blue light shining from what appeared to be a metallic craft that had landed in the forest. Other craft hovered silently in the sky above.

Trance-like state

Base Commander Gordon Williams reported that he approached the craft on the ground and communicated with the creatures in it through sign language. Other witnesses told of watching the creatures repair their craft, which had become damaged when it crashed in the forest, and then take off in a huge burst of speed and light.

After the craft had left, the airmen said that they had found themselves in a trance-like state so that general confusion prevailed. Local people also reported that their farm animals and domestic pets had become disorientated and panic-stricken, to the extent that they had been running out on to the roads and colliding with vehicles. There were also accounts that flickering blue and red lights played over the trees throughout

The dark coniferous trees of Rendlesham Forest.

the rest of the night. Some people even said that small creatures with domed heads had been seen wandering through the forest.

Evidence of aliens

Because of the airmen's confused condition at the time, it was difficult to verify exactly what had happened. However, the indisputable fact was that a very strange occurrence had taken place in the forest, one that could not easily be explained. On the next day, forensic tests were carried out over the whole site and some odd facts emerged.

Firstly, there were some marks on the ground where the landing legs of the craft were thought to have been. These gave out very high levels of radiation. Secondly, the treetops in the area had been damaged as though an aeroplane or other large object had crashed through them. And thirdly, a tape recording of the search had been made by an airman at the time and there were strange noises on it.

To this day, why the radiation levels on the site went up and why the trees in the vicinity were damaged remains a mystery. However, some have disputed the veracity of this tape, claiming that it is a hoax. Since

Left: US stealth bomber. Black, triangular and extremely fast and manoeuvrable, could these aircraft be the source of UFO sightings?

the incident, it has also been rumoured that a video recording of the whole event exists. It was supposedly made by one of the airmen who witnessed it from start to finish. Because this material was so sensitive, it is thought that the military confiscated it and that it then became classified information, never to be made public.

Conspiracy theory?

Many believe that the hushing up of the incident was a conspiracy by the United States military, who were attempting to cover up the fact that there had been a nuclear accident at Rendlesham. In order to avoid local panic, and to deflect criticism, the personnel at the air base pretended that some kind of alien landing had taken place. Other commentators have put forward the theory that the event was actually an American attack on a Russian spy satellite and that it was the satellite, not an alien craft, that was brought down in the forest.

Various other conspiracy theories have been put forward. It has been suggested that the strange craft were top secret air force aerospace vehicles, known as TR-3Bs or "Astras". Inside each of these huge vehicles, it is said, is a nuclear reactor that negates the Earth's magnetic field, so that the craft becomes very light.

It can then move quickly and flexibly within the magnetic field it has created. In addition to the "Astras" there are smaller craft with similar capabilities, so the story goes, called TR-3As or "Black Mantas".

Critics of this theory have pointed out that it would be very difficult to house a nuclear reactor in this way, because it would be extremely heavy. This has then given rise to another theory, that the United States military is in possession of alien technology.

Other sightings

There are many other well-documented sightings of "black triangle" UFOs such as the one that is believed to have landed at Rendlesham Forest in 1980. Most of these have been seen in and around the coast of the United States, particularly near air force bases. According to reports, the UFOs are hundreds of feet long, they make no sound and they either hover or fly very rapidly. One of the most significant of these sightings was at Ans, in Belgium, where on 30 March 1990 the local citizens reported seeing a hovering black triangle over the city. Members of the Belgian Air Force pursued the craft but were not able to keep up with it. They later issued a report admitting that they could not identify the phenomenon. Similarly, on 13 March 1997 in Phoenix, Arizona, citizens noticed "black triangle" craft forming a "V" in the sky. Later, the Air Force reported that what people had seen were flare tests, but this seemed highly unlikely.

Today, the consensus seems to be that such aircraft do actually exist. The Belgian Air Force has evidence of the "black triangle" aircraft that visited Ans that day in the shape of radar tracking, photographs and film. What we still do not know, however, is where the craft come from, who they belong to, how they function and why they appear. Could the black triangles, as some suggest, be evidence of top-secret, advanced US military technology? Are they perhaps signs from an underground, possibly terrorist group, who want to display their might in this way? Or could they indeed be visitations from extra-terrestrial beings? At present, and for the foreseeable future, the mystery remains.

CROP CIRCLES: ALIEN VISITORS OR LOCAL HOAXERS?

A crop circle of flattened wheat in Turin, Italy.

The mysterious appearance of circular patterns in cornfields first hit the headlines during the 1970s, when several of them appeared in England. After these sightings, many people around the world began to report the occurrence of curious, and in some cases very beautiful, patterns in paddy fields and pine forests as well as on snow-covered hills. Critics immediately dismissed the circles as hoaxes and, indeed, some individuals came forward claiming that they had made the circles as a prank.

However, on closer inspection, it became clear that the phenomenon could not be explained so easily. Many aspects of it were very puzzling. For example, the circles typically appeared rapidly; their patterns were complex and very accurate, as though drawn by a compass; and the biological structure of the plants that formed them had changed. Eminent scientists began to conduct research into crop circles and they came up with numerous theories as to how such phenomena could occur. For example, magnetic fields and different types of geological formation could be affecting the plants, causing them to flatten and change.

Yet, to date, no one has come up with a conclusive theory that explains how crop circles have come about. The popular belief that they are evidence of extra-terrestrial beings, perhaps messages to humanity from a higher intelligence on a different planet, continues to predominate.

The first crop circles

Within the ancient folklore of Britain and Northern Europe can be found stories of circles in grass or cornfields. They were thought to be caused by elves and fairies and they could cause disaster if people trod on them. A sixteenth-century woodcut shows a picture of a monstrous creature making a circle in a corn field. However, there are various interpretations of the image and it could well refer to an entirely imaginary event. The first scientific evidence did not appear until the twentieth century, when aerial surveys revealed what were then termed "crop marks" which were thought to be caused by changes in the soil. Many of the sites were investigated and archaeological finds were made, but little attention was paid to the "crop marks" themselves.

Flying saucers

It was not until 1972 that two men, Arthur Shuttlewood and Bryce Bond, reported

Crop circle near the Iron Age burial mound of Silbury Hill in Wiltshire, England. Although there is much anecdotal evidence for the mysterious properties of crop circles, there is very little that is scientifically verifiable.

seeing a crop circle appear before them on a moonlit night at a place called Star Hill, near Warminster in England. They had come out to look for unidentified flying objects, or UFOs, which had apparently been seen many times in the area over a period of ten years or so. Instead, an imprint on the vegetation suddenly materialized before their eyes, opening up like a fan.

After that, many witnesses from around the world, from Japan to the Soviet Union, came forward with similar stories. Apart from the circles, they also told of having seen aircraft and beams of light and heard a high trilling sound. Reported sightings of crop circles increased in number, until they reached the current figure of over 9,000. There are thought to be many more that go unreported each year.

Doug and Dave

Doug and Dave were pranksters who came forward to announce that they had created the crop circles. They claimed that all of them had been made using planks of wood, string and a baseball cap. However, as more complex patterns were reported it became clear that Doug and Dave could not possibly have made such complicated circles. Moreover, because reports were coming in from all over the world, it was hard to explain how they had been in so many places at the same time. In the end, Doug and Dave had to admit that they were not responsible for all the crop circles that were being reported.

Genuine formations

Once the formations had been looked at scientifically, it began to become clear that human beings could not possibly have made them. When plants from the circles were analyzed under the microscope, it was noticed that their biological structure had changed. Not only this, but nodes on the plant stems

The ancient stone circle of Stonehenge is thought to be erected in a significant position in the earth's magnetic field; could crop circles be caused by this powerful network of invisible forces?

appeared to have been blown open in a way that was consistent with them having been heated up. In many cases, otherwise brittle stems were bent but not broken, something that would have been impossible for human beings to do by hand.

Another odd aspect of the formations was that they seemed to alter the magnetic field of the area, so that camera crews filming them suddenly discovered that their equipment was not working. Compasses, mobile phones and batteries also stopped working when they were close to the formations. Aircraft flying above them also reported equipment failure. People living in villages that were close to where circles appeared often told of power cuts, cars failing to start, and animals refusing to walk across or near the circles.

What causes circles?

Most people prefer not to believe that little green aliens travelling around the planet in flying saucers are responsible for the happenings, so a variety of other explanations have been sought. Archaelogists, geologists, and others have pointed to the fact that crop circles often occur over the Earth's magnetic energy lines, which are also known as ley lines. Early humankind often built structures in these places: Stonehenge is just one example. Recent thinking suggests that eddies in the Earth's magnetic field cause crops to flatten and that other environmental factors, such as underground water tables, may make the nodes of plant stems swell up as if heated.

However, this by no means accounts for the appearance of all crop circles, especially the very complex ones. There remains a great deal of controversy over whether the most spectacular crop circles occur naturally, whether they are the work of human beings, or whether they are evidence of alien intervention. It is certainly true that many groups of artists and nature lovers make crop circles, either because they believe that they have a healing effect on the human psyche or because they feel that they are beautiful to look at. However, many have argued that such activity cannot account for every instance of the phenomenon.

Thus, until scientists come up with a completely persuasive explanation for the way in which crop circles suddenly appear on our landscape, enthusiasts will continue to believe that they are the result of supernatural forces. Not little green men, perhaps, but forms of life that, as yet, we know nothing about.

THE MEN IN BLACK

Who are the men in black? Legend has it that these elusive figures are a group of agents that materialize whenever an unidentified flying object appears or any other extraterrestrial occurrence takes place. Their task is to harass or frighten witnesses into denying all knowledge of what has happened. The conspiracy theory that lies behind the idea of the men in black is that alien beings are threatening our planet and want to hide the information from the public. Alternatively, it has been suggested that the men in black are government agents who also wish to suppress the truth.

According to the theory, the government agents or "MIBs" are usually dressed in black suits and display behaviour which is unusual and, possibly, non-human. They threaten witnesses and confiscate photographs, video tapes, and any other means of recording a sighting. In some cases, their black suits have been described as made of a strange shiny fabric which witnesses have not seen before. They have also been described as "mechanical", with monotonous voices and robotic movements.

Some reports even attest to the fact that their faces are not like human faces but have odd slanted eyes and high cheekbones. They are said to travel in threes most of the time, but they have occasionally been reported as travelling alone.

MIBs, so the story goes, drive new Lincolns or Cadillacs, often with the headlights off, and the inside of the cars is lit with a strange green or purple light. The licence plates of the cars are false and there are sometimes odd emblems on the doors. Occasionally, the MIBs arrive in black helicopters and tail witnesses of UFO happenings, intimidating them into giving up any evidence they might have.

First sightings

Since the earliest times, there have always been accounts of emissaries from the gods, or from devils, who disguise themselves to do their masters' business on Earth. In particular, demons were said to wear black, usually sporting the fashions of the day, and to ride about in black carriages in a similar way to the Men in Black of today's urban

Do the Men in Black suppress evidence of alien life?

tales. An eighteenth-century Norwegian story tells of a young girl who was travelling with her grandmother to meet the devil (who turned out to be her grandfather!) and who, on the way, met three men dressed in black. Another, from the early twentieth century, tells of a religious cult that was centred around a woman named Mary Jones. Its members reported seeing strange lights in the sky and encountering "dread apparitions" in the night, including men who were dressed in black.

There has also been speculation among some ufologists that mythical figures from the past, such as Elizabethan and Native American "black men" or nineteenth-century evil travelling salesmen, could in fact have been "Men in Black" who were travelling the earth in order to silence those who had witnessed extraterrestrial events.

The first modern sighting, however, took place in 1947, when a sailor named Harold Dahl reported seeing six unidentified flying objects at a place called Maury Island near Tacoma, Washington. Dahl, who was with his son and his dog, took some photographs. His dog was reportedly killed when some hot sparks from the UFOs landed on the boat. Next day, a man called at his home and took him out to a diner for breakfast. The man, who was tall and dark and wearing a black suit, pumped him for details of the sighting and gave him a severe warning not to tell anyone of it – otherwise his family might be harmed. Later, Dahl claimed that the sighting was a hoax. This was apparently an attempt to follow the MIB's orders, but it caused some confusion and many began to doubt the veracity of his story.

Albert K. Bender

One of the earliest people to pick up on the story was Albert K. Bender, director of the "International Flying Saucer Bureau" and editor of a UFO newsletter entitled *The Space Review*. In a 1953 article, Bender alleged that he had acquired information about flying saucers but was unable to print it and warned that anyone who had similar information was in danger. Issues of *The Space Review* then ceased. Later, Bender explained what had happened. He said that he had been visited by three men in dark suits who had told him the secrets of UFOs and then intimidated him into silence.

After Bender's story was made public, controversy arose around the question of whether or not the "Men in Black" story had been dreamed up by UFO enthusiasts to cover up the fact that they had very little evidence for their stories. Sceptics pointed out that having government or alien agents harass UFO witnesses into silence was a very handy device for explaining why concrete information was not forthcoming. The ufologists, such as writer Gray Barker, Bender's friend, countered by alleging that "sinister men" were suppressing the real story of what was going on in the extraterrestrial world.

Return of the Men in Black

In 1976, a visit from a "man in black" was reported in Maine, by Dr Herbert Hopkins, who had been told about a UFO sighting in the area. According to Hopkins, the man was dressed in a smart black suit but looked extremely strange, with a pale face and bright red lipstick. He threatened Hopkins in a slow, monotonous voice, telling him not to publicize the UFO encounter in any way. He then walked out, leaving Hopkins in a trance-like state.

Four years later there was another visit, this time to Peter Rojcewicz, a folklorist, while he was in the library at Pennsylvania University. A tall man with a dark face, dressed in a black suit, came up behind him and began

Men in Black: Tommy Lee Jones confronts an alien in the film of the same name.

to question him about his studies. Rojcewicz told the man that he was researching UFO encounters, whereupon the man became angry but then calmed down. After he left, Rojcewicz became panicky and went to find help, but there seemed to be nobody around. Later, he realized that there had been people in the library all along, but he had not been able to see them.

Who are the MIBs?

According to US government sources, there is some evidence to suggest that people who have witnessed UFO activity have sometimes been harassed. It is thought that ordinary members of the public have sometimes posed as government officials and intimidated witnesses. In one case, witness Rex Heflin of Santa Ana, California, took photographs of a UFO in 1965, which were published. He later told of receiving a visit from two men who claimed to be representatives of the North American Aerospace Defense Command. They asked for the negatives of the photographs and took them away, never to return them.

Although this case was well documented, there were thought to be many inconsistencies in Heflin's account and to date there is little concrete evidence to suggest that the "Men in Black" actually exist. One complicating factor is that those who claim to have been visited by them often report themselves to have been in a trance-like mental state both during the encounter and after it. This has led some commentators to believe that instead of having been visited by MIBs, the "witnesses" have actually been undergoing some kind of mental crisis which has impaired their state of mind, so that they imagined the whole event.

Another explanation, advanced by the pro-UFO lobby, is that government officials have in fact dressed up in strange clothes in order to discredit the stories of UFO witnesses. Others suggest that the MIBs are in fact alien-human hybrids whose job it is to cover up any trace of alien activity on Earth. Whatever the truth, it seems that these visits have a long history – whether as real events, or as stories that have moved from the folklore of the past to present-day urban mythology – and they look set to continue in the future.

THE MOON LANDINGS

I t is one of the iconic images of the past century: Neil Armstrong emerging from Apollo 11 and uttering the immortal words "That's one small step for man, one giant leap for mankind" – words so apt that they seemed to have been scripted. But what if the whole thing actually was scripted? What if the moon landings never really happened, but were mocked up in a film studio as a propaganda exercise?

That is precisely the belief of an increasing number of Americans. It is an apparently outlandish conspiracy theory that was ridiculed when it first appeared in the early 1970s but has slowly gained credence ever since. After Watergate, Americans became immeasurably more cynical about their government. So when the 1978 film *Capricorn One* portrayed a NASA attempt to fake a landing on Mars, many were prompted to suspect that the film was actually based on inside information. Since then opinion polls have consistently indicated that millions of Americans have their doubts about the moon landings. These doubts were fanned by a Fox Documentary made in 2002, which gave the conspiracy theorists the chance to put their case.

Walking on the moon: Buzz Aldrin's gold-plated visor mirrored the Eagle landing module and Neil Armstrong, who took most of the pictures.

That the astronaut is brightly lit when he is in the shadow of the lander proves for many people the presence of a second light source – an impossibility on the moon. The effect is, however, caused by the reflection of light from the ground.

Were the landings faked?

So what is that case? What is it about the moon landings, watched by millions at the time and for many years after seen as evidence of one of mankind's supreme achievements, that makes the conspiracy theorists suspicious?

Perhaps the best known questions posed by the conspiracy theorists are to do with the photographs of the landings. Why does the American flag appear to be waving in the wind when the moon has no wind? And why are there no stars visible in the sky? Not only that, why do photographs that purport to be taken miles apart appear to have identical backgrounds?

So what explanations can NASA, or anyone else, offer to explain these apparent anomalies? Well, quite a few. Taking them in order: the flag is apparently waving because it had just been unwrapped and then twisted as the flagpole was screwed into the ground. The reason no stars are visible is because the cameras that were used were set for quick shutter speeds, in order not to over-expose the film in the very bright light. The dim light of the stars simply does not have a chance to show up on the film. This same effect can easily be observed on Earth. If you take a picture of the night sky with the camera set for a bright sunny day then the stars will be invisible. The allegation that the backgrounds are identical in different photographs does not stand up to detailed analysis either. A careful comparison of the backgrounds that are claimed to be identical in fact shows significant changes in the relative positions of the hills.

It is just the same on Earth, where a mountain range will appear in much the same place in the backgrounds of photographs taken several hundred feet apart.

Why no blast crater?

The photographs are just one set of issues that have been raised by the conspiracy theorists, however. Some of their other questions deal with more mechanical matters.

Why was there no blast crater visible following the lunar landings? Why did the launch rocket not produce a visible flame? How did the spaceship and its crew survive the journey through the Van Allen radiation belt?

Here are the official scientific responses. There was no blast crater for the simple reason that the Lunar Modules braked before landing, rather than crashing violently into the moon's surface. In any case, their impact was diminished by the much weaker gravity on the moon. There was no visible flame because the Lunar Module used hydrazine and dinitrogen tetroxide, propellants chosen for their ability to ignite upon contact and without a spark. Such propellants happen to produce a nearly transparent exhaust. As for the Van Allen belt, the mission was well prepared for this. The orbital transfer trajectory from the Earth to the Moon through the belts was selected to minimize radiation exposure so that the spacecraft moved through the belts in just thirty minutes. The astronauts were protected from the radiation by the metal hulls of the spacecraft. The dosage received by the astronauts was no more than that gained from a chest X-ray.

Moon rocks

Finally, one particularly complex part of the conspiracy theory has to do with the question of the moon rocks. These are usually seen as the ultimate proof that the moon landings did indeed take place. How else could these rocks, completely different to anything seen on Earth, have come into the possession of NASA? Conspiracy theorists point to the Antarctic expedition of Wernher von Braun, two years prior to the Apollo mission. According to this theory, this mission was used to collect lunar meteorite rocks that could be used as fake moon rocks in a hoax. Von Braun was susceptible to pressure from the authorities. He would have agreed to the conspiracy in order to protect himself from recriminations over his past as a former Nazi.

Well it is a nice theory and it does have some scientific rationale. There are indeed lunar meteorites to be found in Antarctica. However, the first meteorite identified as a lunar meteorite was not found until 1981, a decade after the moon landings. It was only identified as such because of its similarity to the lunar samples returned by Apollo, which in turn are similar to the few grams of material returned from the moon by Soviet sample return. The total collection of identified Antarctic lunar meteorites presently amounts to only about 2.5 kilograms, less than one per cent of the 381 kilograms of moon rocks and soil returned by Apollo. Furthermore, the detailed analysis of the lunar rocks by many different scientists around the world shows no evidence of their having been on Earth prior to their return.

For every point raised by the conspiracy theorists there seems to be a rational scientific explanation. So is there any likelihood that America faked the moon landings? Not really. As scientists have pointed out, given the amount of work it would have taken to fool the world on such an epic scale it would have been easier to just go to the moon.

US geologist and astronaut Harrison Hagan Schmitt takes rock samples from the surface of the moon during America's last lunar landing mission of the 20th century, Apollo 17, December 1972.

THE HOLLOW EARTH

From the earliest times, theories about life under the Earth have abounded. In Ancient Greece, an underworld peopled by the dead was envisaged, which was known as Hades, while Christian mythology conceived of a fiery subterranean place where the damned were sent to endure eternal torture. We know it as Hell. Different versions of these beliefs feature in many ancient religions the world over. But in modern times, there have also been many eminent thinkers and scientists, as well as fiction writers, who have picked up the idea. They describe a "hollow" Earth, often peopled by a prehistoric race, that is reached by a network of subterranean tunnels. Today,

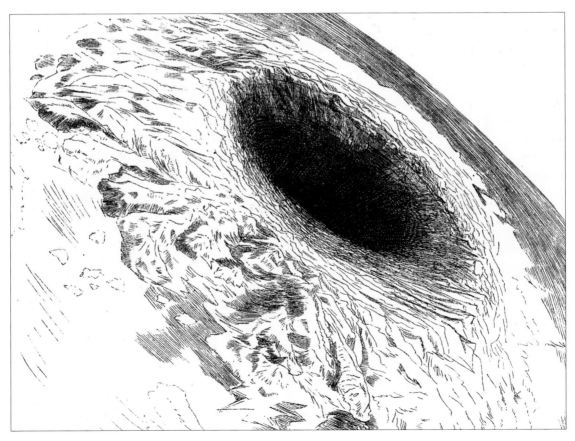

A 19th-century drawing illustrating the theory that a huge opening into the Earth was to be found at the North Pole.

few believe that the Earth really is hollow, or that human beings live at the centre of it, but the idea of a different world underground, where some forms of life exist, still excites the imagination. Recent developments in science have shown that such a notion is not merely the stuff of science fiction.

Halley's inner spheres

In 1692, the renowned English astronomer, Edmund Halley, came up with the idea that the Earth was hollow. As the man responsible for plotting the path of the comet named after him, Halley's opinion was taken seriously. He was an eminent man of science, after all. According to his theory, the reason that the Earth's magnetic field sometimes showed inexplicable variations was because there were other magnetic fields around it, causing opposing gravitational pulls. Halley came up with a new model of the Earth, in which four inner spheres were stacked inside each other. He also advanced the idea that each of these was lit by a luminous gas. The aurora borealis, or Northern Lights, was evidence of this gas, he claimed. This is how the gas looked when it was escaping at the North Pole, where he believed the Earth's crust had thinned. Halley also believed that the spheres could well be inhabited, although he did not specify by what exact forms of life.

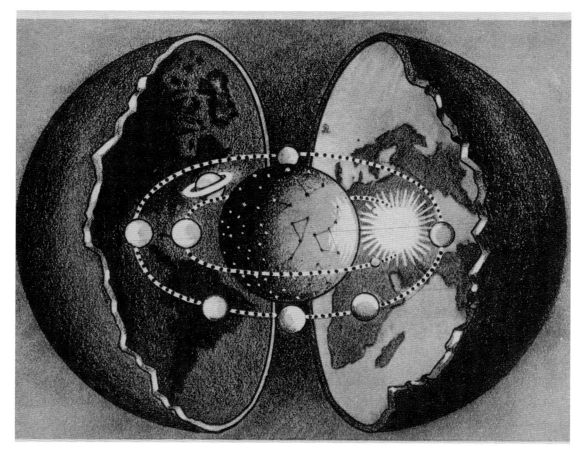

Our hollow Earth: This illustration demonstrates how we actually live on the inside of our globe, looking inwards to the sun and other planets of the solar system.

Next, a Swiss mathematician named Leonhard Euler proposed that instead of several spheres there was only one, which was at the centre of the Earth. This, he thought, was lit by an inner sun that allowed an advanced civilization to prosper there. Today there is some dispute as to whether Euler actually claimed this to be the case, or whether he was merely raising the possibility as a "thought experiment". Whatever the case, his ideas inspired several other thinkers. One of these was another mathematician, a Scotsman called Sir John Leslie, who went on to claim that there were two suns, Proserpine and Pluto, that lit the subterranean realms at the Earth's core.

United States expedition

During the nineteenth century, the idea of a "hollow Earth" became popular among would-be explorers, several of whom suggested making expeditions to find this lost world. In 1818, John Cleves Symmes, a businessman, began to raise money to support an expedition to the "hole" at the North Pole where he believed that the inner spheres of the Earth could be entered. He died before the expedition could take place but, in 1838, a newspaperman called Jeremiah Reynolds took up the challenge, agitating for the United States government to send out a force, which they did in that year. The Wilkes Expedition, as it was called, did not find the alleged hole, but over a period of years they brought back a great deal of useful information about the continent that came to be called Antarctica.

The next proponent of the hollow Earth theory was William Reed, whose book, *Phantom of the Poles*, was written in 1906. Seven years later, Marshall Gardner wrote *A Journey to the Earth's Interior*, and also made a working model of the Earth's core as he envisaged it. When an extinct species of woolly mammoth was found frozen in the ice in Siberia, Gardner advanced the idea that it had strayed out of the inner zone by passing through the hole at the Earth's pole. According to him, all manner of extinct animals wandered about this subterranean world and here was the evidence for it.

Since that time, new generations of writers have come up with the idea of life in this "hollow Earth": from prehistoric animals to a race of enlightened human beings. It has also been claimed that entrance can be gained to this subterranean civilization through holes in the Earth – in Antarctica, Tibet, Peru, and the United States. Not only this, but some believe that UFOs and other extra-terrestrial phenomena emanate from this underworld.

The cult of Koresh

One of the most notorious "hollow Earth" theorists was Cyrus Read Teed, who took the theory one step further by claiming that the Earth was a completely hollow sphere, with a great human civilization living inside it. He founded a cult in Florida and declared himself to be Koresh, a Messiah, before he died in 1908. Outlandish as his ideas sounded, some aspects of physics and mathematics could be employed to support them and a few scientists continued to investigate his ideas after his death.

By the end of the nineteenth century, and well into the twentieth, claims about the existence of a highly developed, ancient civilization under the Earth's crust continued to abound. Not surprisingly, the idea of a master race proved especially popular among Nazi sympathizers. There was even a theory that Adolf Hitler had escaped to join them – via Antarctica in spacecraft – after his defeat in the Second World War and was still alive many years later.

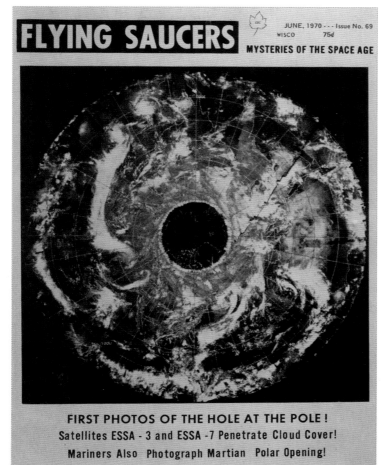

FLYING SAUCERS

JUNE, 1970 - - - Issue No. 69
WISCO 75¢

MYSTERIES OF THE SPACE AGE

FIRST PHOTOS OF THE HOLE AT THE POLE !
Satellites ESSA - 3 and ESSA -7 Penetrate Cloud Cover!
Mariners Also Photograph Martian Polar Opening!

An extremely crudely doctored satellite photograph of the Earth, claiming to show the "Hole at the Pole". The fact that both poles have been visited on several occasions does not appear to dismay proponents of the hollow earth theory at all.

Journey to the centre of the Earth?

Ironically, one of the most persuasive versions of the "hollow Earth" theory came not from a scientist but from an adventure writer: Jules Verne. In his famous book *Journey to the Centre of the Earth*, published in 1864, Verne described a network of tunnels that led from the Earth's surface to underground caves where prehistoric beings live in an underground sea. For many years, scientists thought that such an idea was ridiculous and that nothing could live that far underground, away from the sun. However, recent research has shown that, in fact, there are underground passages leading far into the Earth and that more forms of life flourish there than was previously thought possible. For example, rock-eating bacteria and various kinds of insects such as millipedes and scorpions have been found in places over a mile below ground. No prehistoric creatures such as plesiosaurs have been sighted as yet and there has definitely been no sign of a master race of highly evolved human beings. However, after discovering these simple forms of life deep under the Earth's crust, who knows for certain what else awaits us as science progresses and we journey further into the centre of the Earth?

CHAPTER FOUR:
COVER-UPS

The chaos and confusion of war inevitably produce whole rafts of conspiracy theories, often for the excellent reason that there are, in fact, conspiracies happening at all levels and on all sides. But conspiracy theories also abound in times of relative peace, and perhaps the most readily believed are those involving politicians, whatever their party allegiance. One reason for this may be the number of political cover-up theories which have been demonstrated to be true.

ADOLF HITLER: DID HE ESCAPE?

The standard account of Adolf Hitler's death is that on 30 April 1945 he committed suicide in his Berlin bunker, shooting himself in the head and possibly also taking a capsule of cyanide. With him was Eva Braun, the mistress he had married on the previous day. After their deaths, both bodies were taken into the garden outside by their few remaining friends, doused with petrol, burned and buried in shallow graves. The bodies were later identified by Soviet forces and a hasty autopsy was performed on the remains.

Today, there are those who continue to question this account. Why were the bodies disposed of in this way? Could it be, perhaps, that there were in fact no bodies, and that Hitler and Eva Braun had escaped from the bunker to carry on the Nazi campaign from a secret hide-out? If so, where did they go? Was it to the Bavarian Alps, to South America, or even to New Swabia in the Antarctic?

At the time, several important figures, including Joseph Stalin, believed that Hitler had escaped the bunker and was still alive and active somewhere in the world. As the years went by, the conspiracy theories became more bizarre as links were made with Nazi mythologies about the Aryan race. Some suggested that Hitler had disappeared into the hollow earth, or had travelled with aliens to the star Aldebaran, from where he continues to conduct a campaign to take over the planet Earth.

Far-fetched as some of these theories might be, it is not surprising that there has been a good deal of speculation about the issue. The fact that Hitler's body was so hastily disposed of by the Soviet authorities, and that a satisfactory autopsy was never performed, has meant that we will probably never know the exact circumstances of the death of one of the most notorious leaders in history.

The final solution

In the months leading up to the fall of the Third Reich, Hitler, Eva Braun and his top officials retreated to the so-called "Führerbunker" in Berlin to await their final defeat. By the time the Soviet forces had reached Berlin, Hitler was preparing to commit suicide. He first married his long-term mistress Eva Braun in what must have been one of the most dismal wedding ceremonies ever to take place, using a small map room in the bunker to do so. He then made a will. On the next day, he and his wife said goodbye to their friends and staff, who included Martin Bormann and the Goebbels family. The couple then retreated to Hitler's study, where Bormann and Hitler's valet Heinz Linge later found them lying dead on the sofa. According to their testimony, Hitler was wounded in the head and a pistol lay on the floor. Braun showed no signs of having been shot and was assumed to have taken cyanide.

Linge then told of how he and others on Hitler's staff, including SS guards, took the bodies out to a nearby garden, poured petrol over them, burned them and tried to bury them. However, they could not complete the burial because the Soviet forces were encroaching.

False autopsy

The remains of the bodies were found by Soviet troops from a unit known as the "79th Smersh". The unit, under a forensic pathologist, conducted an autopsy, hoping to discover the cause of death. In order to do so, they used dental records from Hitler's dentist Hugo Blaschke. The pathologist found traces

Opposite: *Germany's leader Adolf Hitler meets young members of the Hitler Youth in Berlin on 20 April 1945, some 10 days before he committed suicide in the last hours before the Russians captured the city.*

of cyanide in both bodies and pronounced that Hitler and his wife had died of cyanide poisoning. The results were made public on 16 May 1945.

However, Hitler's staff continued to attest that the Führer had shot himself, a death that perhaps seemed more dignified to them than self-poisoning. Their claims could not be ignored and the Soviet authorities finally had to accept that the autopsy had been wrong. Embarrassed by the incompetence of the Soviet army over such an important matter, Stalin issued an extraordinary statement on 9 June 1945, to the effect that the remains of Hitler's body had not been found and that he had probably escaped.

Where did he go?

Stalin and the Soviets made a number of conflicting statements over the question of Hitler's body, so that in the end none of their accounts could be believed. At different times, for example, they alleged that Hitler had escaped; that he was being held alive in prison in the Soviet Union; and that they had possession of Hitler's corpse. Not surprisingly, rumours began to abound and sightings of Hitler began to be reported. He was thought, for a time, to be hiding in a secret Nazi stronghold deep in the Bavarian Alps, along with Martin Bormann, Artur Axmann (the head of the Hitler Youth), and Ludwig Stumpfegger (Hitler's doctor). However, when Axmann was captured, he maintained that Hitler had shot himself, while it appeared that Bormann and Stumpfegger had been shot by troops while attempting to break out of Berlin as the Russians closed in.

In the years after World War II, it was believed that an organization of former SS

Photograph reputed to show Adolf Hitler's corpse in his ruined underground bunker. The picture is claimed to have been taken by a close member of Hitler's staff who was in the bunker when he shot himself.

men, ODESSA, masterminded the operation to help fugitive ex-Nazis settle in other countries, especially South America. There were those who believed that Hitler was hiding in Argentina and others who thought that he was holed up in Spain. There was even a theory that he was living in a moated castle in Westphalia.

Hitler returns?

Harder to credit were the theories that Hitler had travelled to Antarctica and had resumed his earlier career as an artist. He was purportedly painting the frozen landscapes of his new home while planning his next attempt at world domination. Allied to this theory was the notion that he had descended, through a portal at the Pole, to a hollow earth zone populated by an alien master race who were about to take over the planet. Bizarre as these ideas might seem, they were not new to Nazi ideology and, in fact, attempts had been made to establish bases in Antarctica in the early days of the Third Reich. Heinrich Himmler had also championed the cause of Nazi mythologies of the Aryan race and, during his lifetime, Hitler had been revered by some Nazis as a saviour sent by God.

Of course, after Hitler's death – or disappearance – deification was only a short step away. A cult known as "esoteric Hitlerism" grew up: in India, where Savitri Devi and Subhas Chandra Bose claimed that Hitler was a follower of the God Vishnu, sent to restore the Aryans to their former glory; and in South America, where Miguel Serrano put forward the theory that Hitler was planning an imminent return. According to Serrano, Hitler was hiding in Shambhala, a subterranean headquarters in Antarctica, with a master race called the Hyperborean gods. He would eventually emerge to fight the Jews once more and institute a Fourth Reich.

The reality

Today, all that remains of Hitler's body is a skull fragment with a bullet hole in it that was found at the Führerbunker and a section of his jaw that was used for dental identification in the autopsy. Rumour has it that Stalin once owned the skull fragment and used it as an ashtray, in a gesture of ultimate triumph over his former enemy. However, it is now in the Moscow Archives.

But the doubts still linger on. Why do the Russian authorities repeatedly refuse to perform DNA tests on the fragments? Why did they secretly dispose of the rest of Hitler's remains? In modern times, few believe that Hitler is currently hiding underground waiting to unleash Nazi terror on the world once again – he would be over a hundred and thirty if he were! – but a question still hangs over the exact circumstances of his death. It is certainly possible that we do not know the full story of what happened, even to this day. While that remains the case, conspiracy theories about the death of Adolf Hitler will continue to proliferate.

The notion that Hitler fetched up in Antarctica is far-fetched to say the least.

THE BOMBING OF PEARL HARBOR

Three stricken US battleships in Pearl Harbor on 7 December 1941. Left to right: USS *West Virginia*, severely damaged; USS *Tennessee*, damaged; and USS *Arizona*, sunk.

One of the most damaging military attacks in history was the bombing of Pearl Harbor on the morning of 7 December 1941. On that day, Japanese planes flew over the United States air bases on the island of Hawaii and bombed them all, including the ships anchored at Pearl Harbor. The greatest tragedy was the sinking of the battleship USS *Arizona*, which blew up and sank with over 1,000 sailors aboard. Nineteen other ships were destroyed, as well

as many aircraft, and more than 2,000 military personnel were killed that day.

Questions began to be asked in the aftermath of the attack. Why were the intelligence systems of the United States military – one of the most powerful forces in the world – unable to predict such a devastating attack from one of the world's less developed countries? (Japan at the time, of course, was not the technologically advanced society that it is today.) And why did Adolf Hitler declare

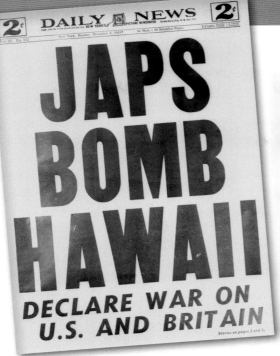

The New York Daily News *of 8 December 1941 announces the Japanese attacks on the American base at Pearl Harbor.*

war on America immediately after the event? Could the attack have been allowed to happen in order to help the American government persuade its people to enter the Second World War? Or is such a betrayal unthinkable?

A set-up job

On the face of it, it did seem odd that the Americans had no idea that the Japanese were about to bomb their fleet. As many people have pointed out, both at the time and afterwards, US signals intelligence was extremely effective. The Office of Naval Intelligence (ONI) and the Army Signal Intelligence Service (SIS) had broken several key Japanese codes and ciphers, including the "Purple" cipher which was thought to relay top security information. It was well known that the militaristic Japanese government was preparing for a large-scale war in order to establish their dominance in Asia, a move that would involve undermining the American forces in the Pacific. So why weren't the Americans on the alert?

Some suggest that the American government, under President Franklin D. Roosevelt, knew perfectly well that the Japanese were about to strike, and secretly informed the top military officials at Pearl Harbor to stand aside and let their ships go down. They point out that while the attack was always depicted as a complete disaster for the American military, in actual fact the loss to the Navy – apart from the loss of life – was only five ships in total. Some of the ships damaged in the attack were later repaired and became operational once more. Also, the Japanese could well have sent more bombers to take out the large fuel supplies on the island, but for some inexplicable reason they did not. Thus, the suggestion is that the bombing of Pearl Harbor by the Japanese was a set-up job that Roosevelt and his advisers colluded in, so that the outraged American public would bay for war, which they subsequently did.

Churchill to blame

Other conspiracy theorists, who find it hard

to believe that the Roosevelt administration could be quite so callous and cynical, particularly in view of the number of casualties sustained, point to Winston Churchill of Britain as a major culprit. They claim that British intelligence knew about the imminent attack and did nothing to inform Roosevelt about it. The British motive, of course, was that they needed help in the war effort to overcome the Nazis, who were allies of Japan under the Axis Alliance (of Germany, Italy, and Japan). By turning a blind eye to Japanese plans for the bombing of the American fleet, the British would help draw the United States into the conflict and thereby gain a powerful new ally. Certainly, the result of the attack was to mobilize public opinion against the Japanese so it made America's entry into the Second World War inevitable.

Plotters or incompetents?

Many believe that the bombing of Pearl Harbor was not so much a conspiracy as a series of errors committed by incompetent military officials. Enquiries into what happened have since revealed that general warnings about Japanese aggression were sent to Pacific commands well before the attack, but that the admiral and the general in Hawaii did not take them very seriously. Later, radio warnings were issued as the Japanese force approached Hawaii, but radio contact was temporarily broken. Also, the FBI had assumed that the Navy were tapping the Japanese Consulate but, as it turned out, their bug had been discovered and disconnected. Another factor in the surprise attack was that the US Navy were not familiar with the new technology of torpedo systems. They believed that their ships could not be torpedoed in the shallow water of Pearl Harbor, which was seen as a protection to their fleet. Unbeknown to them, the Japanese

had developed torpedoes that operated in shallow water – to devastating effect, as the Americans found out.

A number of individuals have come forward over the years, claiming to have information that shows Pearl Harbor to be a conspiracy. "Seaman Z" claims that he overheard signals from the Japanese, but it has since been counter-claimed that the Japanese did not send any signals at the time because they wished to preserve secrecy as they crept up on the American fleet. In the same way, cryptologists have discussed the so-called "Winds Code" signal, claiming that this Japanese weather report was in fact a signal to the Japanese forces to attack Pearl Harbor. However, to date this seems far from conclusive.

What seems likely is that the British and the American intelligence services were both busy with other issues at the time – Britain, in particular, was in the midst of fighting the Germans in World War II! Through a series of bungled communications, therefore, they failed to realize the significance of what was going on in the Pacific. There was simply too much conflict taking place in Europe and other parts of the world for America and the Allies to be able to pay much attention to the threat from Japan and deal with it effectively. In addition, various internal rivalries among the top United States military officials in Hawaii at the time prevented efficient intelligence gathering and swift action to avert the attack.

However, many questions still remain unanswered, so much so that conspiracy theories will continue to abound. After all, it is hard to believe that such a devastating strike on Pearl Harbor's "Battleship Row", as it was called, could be the result of sheer incompetence. But, unlikely as it may seem, that might just be the case.

*Winston Churchill: did he withhold
intelligence of an imminent attack on
Pearl Harbor?*

WATERGATE

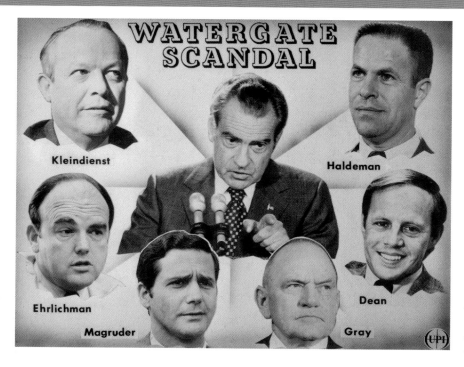

WATERGATE SCANDAL

Kleindienst

Haldeman

Ehrlichman

Magruder

Dean

Gray

Graphic showing the key players in the Watergate Affair, including President Richard Nixon (centre), and White House Counsel John Dean (right).

The Watergate Affair is one of the key conspiracy tales of our time. Not because it is the most outlandish or extraordinary of conspiracies, but because it turned out to be true. What began as a simple burglary turned out to be a scandal that forced the resignation of a United States president. Here was a real conspiracy and it was uncovered layer by layer until the conspirators – all the way up to President Richard Nixon himself – had to resign or face criminal charges. And perhaps the most lasting effect of the episode was to make sure that conspiracy theorists could no longer simply be written off. Previous events like the assassination of John F. Kennedy now looked more suspicious than ever and the conspiracy theorists, once described as crackpots, were

all of a sudden "experts". Never again would the American public simply accept what it was told – even by its president.

The whole extraordinary business began in the early hours of 17 June 1972 at a hotel and office block complex called the Watergate building in Washington, DC. On that day a security guard named Frank Wills noticed a piece of tape being used to hold open a door leading in from the parking garage. Wills removed it, but did not think much of it. He imagined that the cleaning team had perhaps left it there. However, when he returned soon afterwards to discover that someone had put another piece of tape on the door, he decided to call the police. He told them that he suspected that a burglary might be in progress.

The police showed up and at 2.30 a.m. they found five men hiding in an office in the part of the building occupied by the Democratic National Committee. The five men were arrested and were found to include two Cubans, two men with CIA connections and a man named James W. McCord, Jr who was employed as Chief of Security at a Republican organization called the Committee to Re-elect the President. Alarm bells quickly started to ring. This was clearly no ordinary burglary but a politically motivated one.

Then it emerged that this was not the first Watergate break-in. The same team had already broken into the Democratic Campaign HQ and planted bugs there. Part of the reason for their return was to fix some wiretaps that were not working properly. Further alarm bells went off when the telephone number of one E. Howard Hunt was found in McCord's notebook. Hunt was a former White House consultant and CIA employee.

Just a third-rate burglary?

As news of the break-in made its way into the press, questions began to be asked about who in the White House might have known of it. On 19 June *The Washington Post* reported that a Republican security aide was among the Watergate burglars. The former attorney general John Mitchell, head of the Nixon re-election campaign, denied any link with the operation and the White House did its best to play down the significance of the affair. Nixon press secretary Ron Ziegler called it a "third-rate burglary" and the American public found it hard to accept that a President like Nixon – who was way ahead in all the opinion polls – would sanction a wire-tapping operation against his rivals. On 30 August Nixon claimed that White House Counsel John Dean had conducted an investigation into the Watergate matter and concluded that no one from the White House was involved. Nevertheless, press speculation refused to go away.

At his 5 September indictment, James McCord identified himself as retired from the Central Intelligence Agency. The Washington, DC district attorney's office began an investigation into the links between McCord and the CIA, and so too did a couple of young journalists from *The Washington Post*, Bob Woodward and Carl Bernstein. They started to dig deep, aided by leaks from a mysterious anonymous source, known only as "Deep Throat".

During the weeks leading up to the November election *The Washington Post* ran stories reporting that John Mitchell, while serving as attorney general, controlled a secret Republican fund that was used to finance widespread intelligence-gathering operations against the Democrats. Then it reported that FBI agents knew that the Watergate break-in was part of a massive campaign of political spying and sabotage that was being conducted on behalf of the Nixon re-election effort. Still the public took no notice and Nixon was duly re-elected by a landslide.

On 8 January 1973 the original burglars, along with Hunt and another former intelligence operative turned White House security consultant named Gordon Liddy, went to trial. All except McCord and Liddy pleaded guilty and all were convicted of conspiracy, burglary, and wire-tapping. The accused had been paid to plead guilty but say nothing and their refusal to confess to the crimes angered the trial judge John Sirica (known as "Maximum John" because of his harsh sentencing). Sirica handed down thirty-year sentences, but indicated that he would reconsider if the group would be more co-operative. McCord capitulated and wrote a letter to the judge in which he claimed that the defendants had pleaded guilty under duress. He said they had committed perjury at the urging of John Dean, counsel to the President, and John Mitchell, when he was the attorney general.

Secret tapes

By now the "third-rate burglary" had become a major scandal. The revelations just kept coming. On 6 April John Dean, the White House Counsel, began co-operating with the Watergate prosecutors. Nixon promised fresh investigations but began to look like a man engaged in a desperate cover-up. Dean was sacked and other presidential advisers were forced to resign, but the press were still not satisfied. Dean testified that he had mentioned the Watergate break-in to the President thirty-five times. Nixon denied it. But then the existence of tapes that contained all of the President's conversations in the Oval Office was discovered.

Nixon at first refused to release the tapes, but then handed over edited transcripts. Legal moves eventually forced him to hand over the original tapes, but parts of them were discovered to have been erased. Finally,

Congress began to consider an extraordinary move – to impeach the President. At first this seemed impossible but then, with the August 1974 discovery of the "Smoking Gun" tape that proved that Nixon knew of the cover-up operation, the impeachment process looked certain to go ahead. On 8 August Nixon accepted that the game was up and announced his resignation.

And so the most sensational conspiracy case in American history came to its end. Or did it? Today, there are any number of revisionist Watergate theories out there. Some say that the Democrats deliberately set Nixon up. Others suggest that Dean himself was responsible for the whole business and had ordered the break-in to cover up a prostitution scandal in which he was allegedly implicated.

In the final analysis though, it seems that the conspiracy theorists should learn to quit while they are ahead. Watergate was a conspiracy and it went all the way to the top. The guilty parties were even punished for it. What more satisfying end to a major conspiracy could there possibly be?

9 August 1974: Nixon at the White House with his family after his resignation as president.

THE TUSKEGEE SYPHILIS EXPERIMENT

Black American combat airmen, 1942, trained under the Tuskegee Air Program. The Tuskegee Syphilis Experiment was less well-publicized, however.

The Tuskegee Syphilis Experiment, which was run between 1932 and 1972, was one of the most shocking scientific studies ever to take place. In it, 399 black men, most of whom were poor Alabaman sharecroppers, took part in a supposed treatment for "bad blood" which would cure them of illness. They were never told that their illness was syphilis and that – except at the beginning of the study – they were receiving no treatment at all. What was in fact happening was that doctors were studying the ravages of the untreated disease and waiting for them to die so that they could perform autopsies on the corpses. The supposed aim of the experiment was to find out more about the disease and to determine whether it affected black people differently to whites. However, at the end of the study, which continued over several decades, it was suggested that no important knowledge had been yielded. Meanwhile, many men had met their deaths, after terrible illnesses whose symptoms included paralysis, blindness, heart disease, tumours, and insanity. Not only this, many of the men's wives had become infected and their children born with congenital syphilis.

"Special free treatment"

The study was started at the Tuskegee Institute, under the auspices of the United States Public Health Service. Its initial aim was to study a group of black men with untreated syphilis for a period of months and then treat the disease. However, several of the doctors wanted to continue the programme for a longer period and fearing that the men would not want to co-operate if they knew the truth – that they were being studied to see how long it took them to die of the disease – the doctors began to misrepresent what was going on. They began to write to their "patients" advertising "special free treatment", when all they were doing was performing diagnostic tests. These included painful and dangerous lumbar punctures, from which the patients derived absolutely no medical benefits at all.

Shameful ethics

Penicillin became the standard treatment for syphilis in 1947 and there were government initiatives to treat the population in as rapid a manner as possible. Nationwide campaigns invited citizens to attend treatment centres and men who were called up into the army were screened for the disease and given treatment. The subjects of the Tuskegee Syphilis Experiment, however, were excluded from the programme but they accepted the story that they were being treated already. In this way, syphilitic men were prevented from gaining treatment that would have saved their lives.

It was not until 1966 that the story broke in the national press. Peter Buxtun, who worked for the Public Health Service in San Francisco as a venereal disease investigator, became aware of the experiment and wrote to his superiors to inform them of what was going on. However, he was told that the experiment needed to go ahead and that it would not be curtailed until all the subjects had died and the autopsies had been performed. Frustrated by this brush-off, Buxtun went to the newspapers and in 1972 several national newspapers ran stories on the experiment. The experiment was quickly brought to a halt as a result of the adverse publicity and the surviving subjects and their families compensated and promised free medical treatment in the future.

Two years later, legislation was put into effect to regulate medical experiments involving human beings. However, it was not until 1997 that a public apology was made by the President of the United States. In the presence of the five remaining survivors of the study (only eight were left in total) President Clinton formally apologized for the behaviour of the United States government and called it "shameful".

A conspiracy against ethnic minorities

The fact that the study was conducted on black people led many to accuse the scientists who mounted it of racism. However, this was complicated by the fact that several of the staff in charge of the experiment were African-Americans. The experiment was also conducted under the auspices of one of America's most respected black universities, the Tuskegee Institute, set up by Booker T. Washington. The hospital of the university loaned medical facilities to the Public Health Service in order that they could conduct the experiment and local African-American doctors also became involved.

One of the central figures in the drama was a black nurse called Eunice Rivers. She had worked with the subjects for nearly forty years and was trusted by most of them. Defending her behaviour, she claimed that she was simply carrying out the orders of the doctors and was not in a position to diagnose the patients' illnesses.

Ninety-four-year-old Herman Shaw speaks as US President Bill Clinton looks on during ceremonies at the White House in May 1997, in which Clinton apologized to the survivors and families of the victims of the Tuskegee Syphilis Experiment.

Strangely, both black doctors and nurses felt that they were helping solve the problem of venereal disease in the Afro-American community, and they were deeply committed to health programmes that helped the poorest people in their area, Macon County. It was as if they simply could not see that human beings should not be treated in this way, as just a means to an end, even in the cause of supposedly extending medical knowledge.

Also perplexing is the way in which the study was set up. Once it had been dismantled, many questions were asked. Why, for example, had it been thought necessary to find out the differences between the progress of the disease on white people and black people? The study was set up to find out whether it was true that black people experienced cardiovascular problems as a result of syphilis infection, whereas white people were more susceptible to neurological malfunctioning. But how this information would have helped treat the disease remains unclear.

Not only that, but also the scientific methodology in the study was flawed. The investigation was designed to show how the disease progressed when untreated but the subjects had already been treated – with contemporary treatments such as mercurial ointments – in the first few months of the programme, before it was decided to extend the study. The thinking behind the experiment was so unclear and the scientific gains were so questionable that one can only assume that an extraordinary level of, possibly unconscious, racism must have blinded the scientists to the fact that they were treating their subjects in a completely inhuman way.

In several later sociological studies the Tuskegee syphilis experiment was shown to have had an adverse effect on health programmes directed at African-Americans, who unsurprisingly increasingly mistrusted the public health authorities. The episode caused lasting damage and it is remembered as one of the most appalling conspiracies ever to take place in American history.

THE WACO INCIDENT

Over the past thirty years several events have shaken America and made a significant minority of Americans deeply cynical about the behaviour of their own government. Among the most significant of these is the incident that took place at the Branch Davidian compound near Waco, Texas, in early 1993. This culminated in the loss of more than ninety lives as the government appeared to declare war on a tiny religious sect.

The sect in question, the Branch Davidians, were an offshoot of an offshoot of the Seventh Day Adventist Movement. They had been based in a compound called Mount Carmel, outside Waco, Texas since the 1930s. By 1955 the leadership of the group had passed to one Benjamin Roden, who was succeeded in time by his wife Lois. In 1981 a charismatic young man named Vernon Howell joined the group and he soon became a leading light, especially after he began an affair with the much older Lois. A power struggle began between Howell and Lois's son George. George Roden was the initial victor and Howell left the group to start his own splinter group in 1984. Lois died in 1986 and George Roden assumed control for two years until Vernon Howell returned and managed to wrest control back from the increasingly mentally unstable George.

Vernon Howell began to impose his own vision on the sect. He decided that he was a Messiah figure and should be allowed to be polygamous. He was believed to have recruited

David Koresh, Waco Cult Leader, 1993

as many as twelve women as his concubines, some of them the wives of other members and some of them as young as twelve years old. As the Messiah he also exempted himself from the sect's restriction on diet and alcohol. In 1990 he gave himself a new, rather more biblical-sounding, name: David Koresh. His teachings became increasingly apocalyptic with the United States government being denounced continually as Babylonians. The compound was renamed Ranch Apocalypse. The group stockpiled enough food to last for a year as well as large quantities of arms and ammunition. Dealing in guns – legally – also became a significant source of income for the group.

Gradually the activities of the Branch Davidians and their leader started to worry their Texan neighbours. Reports began to appear in the newspapers that Koresh had been accused of abusing children. The Bureau of Alcohol Tobacco and Firearms started taking an interest in their group. When a postman reported a delivery of what appeared to be grenade casings, the investigation intensified and the bureau found evidence of several minor firearms violations.

Rather than simply waiting for Koresh to make one of his regular visits to the city, however, the BATF decided to launch a huge raid on the compound. Scheduled for 28 February 1993 it was meant to be a surprise but news crews had been tipped off and the BATF helicopter flying over the compound shortly beforehand must have warned the residents that something was amiss.

Forced to retreat

The agents approached the compound that Sunday morning in vehicles disguised as cattle trailers. However, the Branch Davidians were not fooled and the situation very quickly got out of control. As the agents approached the compound, shots rang out. It is still not clear who fired first, with both sides accusing the other, but before long a full-scale gun battle had broken out. By the time the shooting ended four BATF agents and five Branch Davidians were dead and many more were injured.

The BATF had been forced to retreat because they had underestimated the firepower and determination of the sect members. The raid had been an unqualified disaster which had been caught on film for the world to see. Still, the government could not back down now, so a siege began immediately, with the FBI soon taking over the leadership from the BATF.

BATF agents enter a building on the compound through a window.

The siege lasted for an amazing fifty-one days. During that time the FBI seemed to employ two distinct tactics. On the one hand, hostage negotiators talked regularly with David Koresh and in the early days of the siege they secured the release of several groups of members, mostly children.

However, although the negotiators were accustomed to hostage situations this one was very different. The remaining people inside the compound did not see themselves as hostages. They were determined to stay with their leader and it became increasingly clear that Koresh was not intending to leave in the near future. At the same time, hostile tactics were also being used. After a while, the electricity was cut off to the compound and later on giant floodlights were trained on the building in order to prevent the occupants from sleeping.

Notoriously, the FBI also played tapes at deafening volume to demoralize the occupants – the sounds on the tapes included Tibetan Buddhist chants, bagpipes, seagulls crying, helicopters, dentists' drills, sirens, dying rabbits, a train, and songs by Alice Cooper and Nancy Sinatra. Such tactics had been seen to be useful in the operation against the Panamanian leader General Noriega a couple of years before, but the Branch Davidians seemed to be made of sterner stuff and the FBI started to run out of patience. The operation was enormously expensive and the eyes of the world were upon it. Surely the might of the American government could not be halted by a handful of religious fanatics?

Up in flames

Eventually, Attorney General Janet Reno approved plans for a final assault. This was launched on Monday morning 19 April. The FBI called the compound to warn the occupants that they would be using tear gas. Armed

vehicles then approached the compound, punched holes in the walls and sprayed tear gas into the building. Still the Davidians refused to leave. Instead, they started firing at the vehicles. Then the telephone was thrown out, a sign that the talking was over. Later, towards noon, as the FBI pondered its next move, the compound went up in flames. Fires were raging and these were soon punctuated by huge explosions. Finally, nine occupants emerged. One woman came out with her clothing in flames and then tried to go back in, but she was restrained by a BATF agent and taken to safety.

It was too dangerous for firefighters to approach the blaze. Even when it appeared to be in its last stages a soldier was shot at when he approached the building. Eventually, however,

Explosions rock the Branch Davidian compound as the FBI and ATF begin their assault.

Evidence for this, however, was at first slight but the dogged investigations of a right-wing maverick named Michael McNulty started to raise embarrassing questions. He would air his findings in two successful films about the affair – the Academy Award nominated *Waco: The Rules of Engagement* and *Waco: A New Revelation*.

Two key allegations are made by McNulty. The first is that the FBI caused the fires. After the event, the FBI had always maintained that it had not used any flammable substance or weapon in its assault on the compound. McNulty discovered, however, that flammable tear gas canisters had been used in the attack. The FBI finally reversed its earlier statements and admitted this in 1999. Secondly, McNulty examined heat-sensitive film of the operation and noticed flashes coming from behind the building. These, he claimed, were muzzle flashes – proof that the FBI had been firing on anyone trying to escape the fire.

Some of McNulty's other charges were supported by rather less documentary evidence. They included the suggestion that soldiers from the Army's super-secret Delta Force participated in the attack; that hand-held grenade launchers were fired at the kitchen and could have ignited the fire; and that a demolition charge was placed on the roof of the bunker which was detonated by remote control.

So how has the FBI responded to these charges? The explosion in the bunker has been blamed on the quantity of arms possessed by the occupants. The use of grenade launchers and the active involvement of Delta Force soldiers (though they were acknowledged to have been present) were both flatly denied.

the compound was razed to the ground and the FBI was able to inspect the damage. They found eighty dead bodies amongst the rubble of which twenty-three were children (fourteen of whom were fathered by Koresh). The body of Koresh himself was identified by his dental records. He had been shot in the head.

This was an operation that had gone about as wrong as it possibly could. The FBI tried to stress that the Branch Davidians had set the fires themselves and so had committed mass suicide, but it was inevitable that the conspiracy theorists would soon get to work.

Deliberate murder?

Essentially the conspiracy theorists were all saying the same thing, that the FBI had deliberately murdered the Branch Davidians.

The aftermath of the siege: the compound is now a burnt-out shell, and over eighty people lie dead in and around its confines.

The flashes on the heat-resistant film were written off as reflected sunlight, with experts pointing out that a muzzle would have to be attached to a human being who would also show up on heat-resistant film. As for the flammable CS gas canisters, the FBI says that they were launched four hours prior to the fire breaking out but, in any case, they had failed to reach their target. This was backed up by a civil jury, Congress, the Court, and the Special Counsel who, in the year 2000, all concluded that the FBI had not caused the fire. The FBI also point out they had introduced bugging devices into the compound which clearly recorded cult members spreading fuel about and preparing to light it.

Tragic consequences

All this, of course, has cut little ice with conspiracy theorists. What they and many other Americans point out was that here was a religious group surrounded by government forces but still going up in flames. The Waco incident made for potent TV images and proved a powerful recruiting aid for the far-right militias.

This incident would bear terrible fruit two years later when, on the anniversary of the Waco deaths, a young man named Timothy McVeigh decided to take vengeance on the government by perpetrating the Oklahoma City bombing.

So, do the conspiracy theorists have a point? Could Waco have been a massive plot by the government against its own people? It seems unlikely, because in the final analysis there is no reason why the government would have actively wanted to bring about the annihilation of this obscure religious cult. What seems far more likely is that this was simply a disastrously badly handled affair. It was less a conspiracy than a shambles. Unfortunately, however, the consequences of the government's actions were tragic, both in the short and the long term.

MIND CONTROL: MKULTRA

One of the most bizarre and disturbing conspiracies of all time was Project MKULTRA. This was the secret name for a series of CIA experiments that took place from the 1950s to the 1970s, which were designed to explore the possibilities of mind control through the use of drugs such as LSD and mescaline. In these experiments, subjects were given mind-altering drugs, often without their prior knowledge, and their subsequent behaviour was then studied.

In several cases the experiments resulted in the death of one or another of the participants and there were many instances of severe, permanently damaging mental illness. However, the CIA continued to conduct the trials until the project was finally exposed. Ultimately, very little useful information about mind control resulted from MKULTRA and it seems that sadism, rather than serious scientific enquiry, was the driving force behind some of the experiments.

Truth drugs

MKULTRA was set up by Allen Dulles, head of the CIA, in 1953, in order to look into the use of mind control techniques. The project was led by Dr Sidney Gottleib, and early research was directed towards trying to find a "truth drug" for use in the interrogation of Russian spies. The project was wide reaching, with over a hundred research programmes, many of which were secret, and experiments were conducted on army and other personnel without their knowledge.

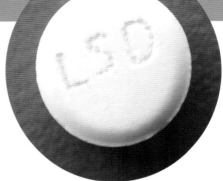

A powerful hallucinogen, LSD was given to subjects of the MKULTRA programme for prolonged periods, sometimes causing permanent mental damage.

In the initial phase of the project, the effect of radiation on the human mind was the main focus of research but, as time went on, interest began to centre on the effect of psychotropic drugs, particularly LSD. As the programmes proliferated, subjects began to be recruited from outside the army and the CIA. Patients with mental illnesses (many of them with minor disorders such as mild depression and anxiety), prostitutes, and other types of individual were often used as guinea pigs. An undeniable element of torture crept into the experiments, as Gottleib began to tie his victims up in straitjackets after administering the drugs. They were often locked in rooms where they could see or hear nothing or tape loops were played to them in an attempt to drive them mad. Gottleib also ordered his subjects to be given enormous amounts of LSD – in one experiment, volunteers were given the drug for a period of over two months, causing many of them to suffer permanent mental damage.

Michael Caine stars in The Ipcress File, *a spy thriller in which mind control through the use of drugs features heavily.*

Operation Midnight Climax

As time went on, the MKULTRA research programmes became ever more bizarre and unpleasant, but they yielded very little in the way of scientific results. One of the most infamous of the experiments was Operation Midnight Climax, in which Dr George Hunter White recruited prostitutes from San Francisco. The prostitutes were asked to administer LSD to their clients without the clients' knowledge. The LSD was put into the victims' drinks and CIA operatives monitored their behaviour through two-way mirrors. No scientific benefits at all accrued from this experiment – the operatives were not trained scientists – and one can only assume that it was set up as a means of satisfying the prurient interests of those who devised it. However, it took more than a decade for this programme to end.

It was later revealed that Dr Gottleib's behaviour as head of MKULTRA was also questionable. He was known to take large amounts of LSD himself and he seemed obsessed with the drug, even though it began to emerge that it was of very little use as a mind control device. Subjects under the influence of the drug behaved erratically and, if anything, became less susceptible to interrogation than they had been without the drug.

Dangerous treatments

Undeterred by the fact that LSD seemed to be useless as a mind-controlling substance, the MKULTRA team went on to perform more and more dangerous experiments on their hapless victims. In some cases, they simultaneously drip-fed a mixture of amphetamines and barbiturates into their subjects, which resulted in extreme mental confusion and sometimes even death. In addition to the use of LSD, amphetamines, and barbiturates the MKULTRA team experimented with other drugs such as heroin, mescaline, marijuana, and alcohol.

Perhaps the worst abuses of all took place in Canada, under the aegis of Dr Ewan Cameron. Dr Cameron had put forward a theory of "psychic driving" in which he claimed that the mind could be erased and then corrected through drugs and other therapies. He conducted experiments in

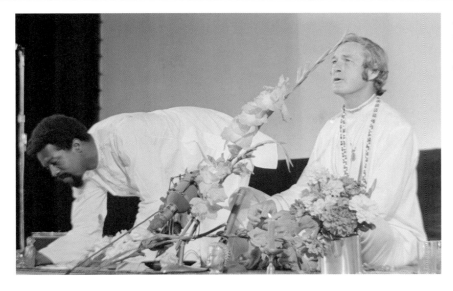

Doctor Timothy Leary, acid guru and main advocate of the use of LSD to gain insight into the world beyond the senses.

Montreal over a period of almost a decade, using a combination of electroconvulsive therapy and drugs, both administered at well above the normal levels. He regularly induced comas in his subjects, sometimes for months on end, while playing them tape loops, supposedly to correct their thinking. Not surprisingly, by the end of his treatment, many of his patients were mentally scarred for life.

Blowing the whistle

It was not until 1974 that the project came under press scrutiny, when an article in *The New York Times* reported on the CIA's history of experimentation on human beings for the purposes of "mind control" research. Several committees were set up to look into what had happened, but they found that much of the evidence had gone missing. Many of MKULTRA's records had been destroyed in order to prevent the truth from ever coming out. Even so, there was enough information to show that the MKULTRA project had been very extensive. Over thirty universities and other institutions had been involved and many of the subjects had been completely

unaware that they were being given drugs. Not only this, but the experiments were mostly completely pointless from a scientific point of view.

It was also revealed that an army scientist, Frank Olsen, had been given LSD without his knowledge as part of an experiment and had later thrown himself out of a window and died. His family later alleged that he was murdered because he knew too much about the CIA's nefarious activities. There were also reports that a professional tennis player, Harold Blauer, had died as a result of being given high doses of mescaline without his consent.

Following these revelations, the United States army was also investigated and a number of shocking cases came to light. They involved subjects who had been given drugs without their consent or knowledge, as a part of so-called experiments. Legislation was enacted to prevent such abuses occurring again and compensation was paid to some of the victims. Nevertheless, the MKULTRA project remains one of the most sinister, and bizarre, state conspiracies ever to have taken place in America, or perhaps anywhere else.

CHAPTER FIVE:
MURDER MYSTERIES

From Agatha Christie's genteel criminals, to the more graphic detective novels of the twenty-first century, a good murder mystery is the book of choice with which to curl up in an armchair for millions of people the world over. And if that murder mystery involves celebrities, sex, politicians, and may in fact be true, that only serves to make it all the more enjoyable!

WHO SHOT JFK?

The assassination of John F. Kennedy on 22 November 1963 has generated more conspiracy theories than almost any other crime in history. This is partly because the crime was such a shocking, dramatic event. As we all know, the President was fatally shot in full view of the public while riding along in an open-topped motorcade, with his wife beside him. But it is also because the hastily assembled Warren Commission, set up just one week after the assassination for the purpose of enquiring into what happened, failed to account for the many perplexing aspects of the crime. The Commission found that a lone gunman, Lee Harvey Oswald, had fired three shots at the President. The first of these missed the motorcade; the second wounded both Kennedy and the Governor of Texas, John B. Connally, who was also riding in the limousine; and the third and final shot hit Kennedy in the head, killing him.

The related conspiracy theories became known as "The Lone Gunman Theory" and "The Single Bullet Theory" (often jokingly referred to as the "Magic Bullet Theory" because it seemed so unlikely that one bullet could penetrate two people). In time, both theories came to be regarded as highly implausible – not only by the experts but by the majority of the American public, who were polled on numerous occasions in order to obtain their opinions on the matter.

To compound the confusions, on 24 November 1963 Jack Ruby, a Dallas nightclub owner, shot Oswald dead while he was in police captivity. Once again, the killing took place in full view of the public. The event prompted a new wave of speculation. How was it that Ruby had found it so easy to flout the tight security surrounding Oswald? Had

The most famous conspiracy of all: President John F. Kennedy and wife Jackie in the limousine that would take Kennedy to his death on Dealey Plaza, Dallas.

First Lady Jacqueline Kennedy leans over to assist her husband who lies on the rear of the car after being shot.

Oswald been swiftly executed in order to prevent incriminating evidence being brought against establishment figures at the trial? And what about Ruby's links to the world of organized crime? Was the Mafia involved in some way with Kennedy's death? Ruby swore that he had been acting on his own, in revenge for the killing, but many disbelieved him. By the time he died of a stroke on 3 January 1967, his motives were still thought by some to be questionable.

The Grassy Knoll

Rumours about the Kennedy assassination persisted throughout the years that followed until, in 1976, the evidence was re-examined by a House Select Committee that was convened for that purpose. This time, the committee found that there were probably two gunmen, not one, and that four bullets were fired: three by Oswald, and one from an unknown gunman hiding in a nearby area that was known as the Grassy Knoll. Many witness reports were collected, some of them conflicting, and evidence was also acquired from people who had photographed, filmed, or recorded the event. However, the report was not conclusive. It merely suggested that a conspiracy of some kind seemed likely, given the probability that

two gunmen were responsible (a theory based on acoustic recordings of the gunshots fired).

A case of foul play?

After the assassination, many troubling facts surrounding the event came to light. For example, the limousine that the President had been travelling in was taken away and cleaned up directly after the shooting, rather than being preserved so that forensic examinations could take place. Also, Kennedy's body should have been inspected by the local coroner according to Texan law, but it was immediately taken to Washington instead. Moreover, the area in which the assassination had taken place, The Dealey Plaza, should have been sealed off by police. The place where Oswald worked, the Texas School Book Depository, should have been closed off also. However, in the event neither place was secured, so vital clues to what really happened might well have been lost. And later, important pieces of evidence were found to be missing, such as the hat that Governor Connally was holding in his hand when he was shot, and the cufflink from his shirt. More shockingly, photographs of Kennedy's autopsy also disappeared.

Much of this could be put down to official incompetence but, after the assassination,

Lee Harvey Oswald is assassinated by nightclub owner Jack Ruby at Dallas police station, 24 November, 1963.

President, Lyndon B. Johnson, appeared to offer a safe pair of hands. He was older, more pragmatic and apparently impervious to the liberal currents running through America during the 1960s.

When Johnson took over, he immediately sent troops back to Vietnam and stepped up anti-communist political propaganda in the United States. The speedy change in foreign and domestic policy confirmed to some observers that the political establishment were behind Kennedy's killing. Oswald was thought to be a decoy figure, a pro-communist who had been hired to shoot the President so that Johnson could take over. The extent of Johnson's personal involvement in the plot remained unclear, but some believed that he had arranged the shooting himself. It also transpired that shortly before he died Kennedy had been thinking of removing Johnson from office, mainly because the Vice President was the subject of four criminal investigations (all of which were dropped after he became the new President). Johnson had more than enough motive to arrange the assassination, it seemed.

there were so many anomalies surrounding the event that a host of conspiracy theories arose to explain what had actually happened. Some of these – like the idea that Kennedy masterminded his own suicide – are difficult to credit. Others, however, such as the theory that right-wing elements of the American establishment wanted Kennedy out of the way, and therefore arranged the shooting, do not seem altogether implausible.

The rival strikes

American foreign policy at the time – which later turned out to be disastrous – was to escalate America's "anti-communist" involvement in Vietnam. Kennedy had shown signs of pulling back from the conflict by recalling United States forces and questioning the scale of human losses that would inevitably ensue. Thus, Kennedy was beginning to be seen as a liability within the political establishment. Conversely, his Vice

Mafia madness

Another theory was that President Kennedy was killed by the Mafia. The Kennedy regime had made it a priority to crack down on organized crime and high-level Mafia leaders were being prosecuted for illegal activities such as gambling, drug running, racketeering, and pimping. There was particular resentment among some Mafia bosses, as they had directed Mafia-linked organizations, such as workers' unions, to run campaigns supporting Kennedy's election. Because they expected to be protected from prosecution once he was in power, so the theory goes, Kennedy's war on organized crime was seen as a betrayal and so he was gunned down in revenge.

It was significant that Jack Ruby, who shot Oswald, had worked for Al Capone as a young man and had continued to be part of the world of organized crime.

According to this theory, Oswald was hired to shoot the President so that it would seem that a communist had done the deed. Oswald was then shot by Ruby, who was posing as a loyal citizen. In this way, Oswald's testimony would not be heard and it would not emerge that it was the Mafia, and not the communists, who had shot one of America's most popular presidents.

Finally, commentators noted that prosecutions of Mafia organizations returned to their normal level after the assassination of Kennedy.

A CIA plot?

Not only the Mafia but the CIA had strong reasons to get Kennedy out of the way. Once in office, Kennedy infuriated the agency by refusing to back the Bay of Pigs invasion in Cuba, which was part of a plot to overthrow the Communist leader Fidel Castro. Kennedy sacked the Director of the CIA, Alan Dulles, and there were constant run-ins between the President and the agency, especially after the failed invasion of Cuba.

The CIA worked very closely with the Mafia, and both organizations saw it as mutually beneficial to oust Castro from Cuba. The CIA's motive was to rid the United States of their closest communist neighbour and the Mafia's motive was to win back control of the organized crime business in Cuba, which they had quickly lost when Castro took control.

Several top Mafia men, aided by the CIA, plotted to assassinate Castro. Thus, Kennedy's perceived reluctance to support their anti-Cuban stance was a constant source of irritation to the CIA and the Mafia.

The FBI boss

The head of the FBI, J. Edgar Hoover, was also suspected of plotting Kennedy's assassination. There was a good deal of mutual animosity between Hoover and the Kennedy clan. Hoover and Johnson, on the other hand, were the best of friends. Hoover was coming up to retirement age and he knew that Kennedy would let him go whereas Johnson, by contrast, would keep him in. Commentators noted that after Johnson became president, he did indeed retain Hoover's services as head of the FBI – "for life".

The other contenders

There are many other theories regarding the culprits in the Kennedy assassination: some of them simple, others labyrinthine. First, there are the "economic issue" conspiracy theories. For example, some think that the oil barons wanted the President dead because he had changed the tax laws regarding oil, which would lose them enormous profits. Others suppose that officials of the US central bank, the Federal Reserve, were worried by the President's plans to stop the counterfeiting of money by backing the currency with precious metals.

Then there are the "political issue" hypotheses. Castro was behind the assassination, it has been said, as a response to the constant attempts by United States agents to murder him. Another theory is that followers of the South Vietnam President, Ngo Dinh Diem, ordered the assassination in

Jackie Kennedy with her second husband Aristotle Onassis. The more outlandish conspiracy theories name both of them as potential culprits in the assassination of JFK.

revenge for his death after the United States plotted a coup against him. Others say that Kennedy was a puppet of the Soviet Union, which then turned against him.

The following theories are more implausible, in the eyes of most people. The first one states that Kennedy was killed in order to avenge the honour of Jacqueline Kennedy, to whom he had been unfaithful on many occasions. Another suggests that Aristotle Onassis ordered Kennedy's murder, along with his friends in the secret Illuminati cabal. Finally, some people imagine that Kennedy did not die at all, but that the whole event was somehow stage-managed to look as though he did. To support this theory, an exchange of bodies would need to have taken place at the autopsy.

Whatever the truth of the matter, some people consider that the Warren Commission's initial findings were questionable and that there were strong pressures to rid the country of a president that threatened to shake up the status quo, both within the government and outside it. Perhaps President Kennedy acted through inexperience and recklessness, as some critics believed, or maybe he had made a serious moral commitment to rid the US of the atmosphere of distrust and fear that had built up as a result of the Cold War, both in terms of domestic and of foreign policy.

For many, Kennedy's death was seen as a tragedy. Whatever his personal failings, he stood as a symbol of hope for a better, more peaceable world, not only for America but for many other countries too. On the day he was killed there were hundreds of troops flying back from Vietnam on his express orders. Had he gone on to withdraw entirely from Vietnam, the Vietnamese and the American public might have been spared one of the most appalling wars in recent history. No wonder, then, that so many intelligent, committed political analysts refuse to let the matter drop and continue to ask to this day: who shot JFK?

MARILYN MONROE: SUICIDE OR MURDER?

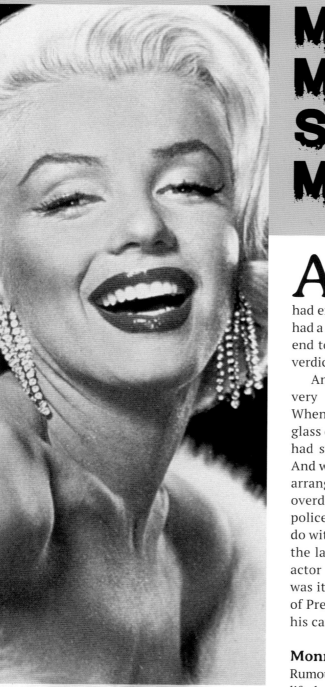

Sex symbol par excellence, Marilyn Monroe charmed her way into ranks of the rich and powerful, but it was not to end well.

At first sight it seemed simple enough. A famous movie actress, whose career was on the skids, took an overdose and died. She had enjoyed a famously turbulent love life and she had a history of suicide attempts. A sad but familiar end to a celebrity's life. That's what the coroner's verdict would ultimately conclude.

An open and shut case? Not really. From the very start there were worrying circumstances. When Monroe's body was found, where was the glass of water she would surely have needed if she had swallowed an overdose of sleeping tablets? And why did her body look as if it had been neatly arranged – quite unlike the usual posture of overdose victims? Why the delay in calling the police and the ambulance? Could it have been to do with the phone calls she made and received on the last evening of her life, including one to the actor and Kennedy intimate Peter Lawford? And was it true that Robert Kennedy, younger brother of President Jack Kennedy, had been seen driving his car away from her house that night?

Monroe's love affairs

Rumours about what had been going on in Monroe's life before she died abounded, and it was only a matter of time before several competing conspiracy theories began to surface. Most of them centred on her involvement with the President. According to

Happy Birthday Mr. President

A HEARTFELT PLEA ON YOUR BIRTHDAY
LET LOVERS BREATHE THEIR SIGHS
AND ROSES BLOOM AND MUSIC SOUND
LET PASSION BURN ON LIPS AND EYES
AND PLEASURES MERRY WORLD GO ROUND
LET GOLDEN SUNSHINE FLOOD THE SKY
AND LET ME LOVE
OR
LET ME DIE!

Rolex watch given to John F. Kennedy by Marilyn Monroe, inscribed with the 'heartfelt plea': 'Let me love or let me die!'

these accounts, Monroe had been having an affair with John F. Kennedy and had threatened to go public on the subject, which would have destroyed Kennedy's political career. Clearly, in those circumstances, the President would have had every reason to have her silenced.

No one suggested that J.F. Kennedy had actually killed Marilyn Monroe with his own hands, so the next step was to determine the identity of the killer. Some named the President's brother, Robert Kennedy. Various witnesses claimed to have seen him visit Monroe during the course of the fatal evening. Could he have gone to plead his brother's case and then – when she refused to stay silent – did he resort to killing her?

Another theory also claims that Robert Kennedy murdered Monroe but that he did not commit the act on his brother's behalf but his own, because he too was having an affair with Monroe. This theory suffers from a lack of evidence and some argue that, even if the two had been lovers, there would have been less for Robert to lose if Marilyn had decided to go public and reveal the liaison.

Mafia men

It was then suggested that the murderer was a hireling of gangster Sam Giancana. According to this theory, Kennedy had turned to his Mafia boss friend for help in the delicate situation he found himself in. Giancana then gladly agreed to send his henchmen in to deal with Monroe. In return, Kennedy was to assist Giancana with projects that were dear to the Mafia's heart, such as the overthrow of Fidel Castro.

As with Robert Kennedy, there were those who suspected that Giancana could have carried out the murder on his own behalf, in a bid to silence Monroe because they too had been having an affair. However, as many have pointed out, if it had been revealed that a mobster had been having an affair with Marilyn Monroe it could only have enhanced his reputation!

Since Monroe's death, the many conspiracy theories that have been advanced have mostly been met with scepticism. Most people are reluctant to believe that the President of the United States, or his brother, could have murdered a legendary movie star in order to protect their reputations. However, it does seem that in the case of Monroe's death – as in the case of the assassination of Kennedy himself – there are plenty of disturbing facts and questions that still need to be answered. Reputable Monroe biographers such as

During a party at the home of movie executive Arthur Krim, Marilyn Monroe stands between Robert Kennedy (left) and John F. Kennedy.

Anthony Summers and Donald Spoto have tended to steer a middle course, suggesting that her death was neither a deliberate murder nor an innocent suicide, but something rather more complex than that.

An accidental overdose?

It is possible that Monroe's death was the result of an accidental overdose. She had been taking a great many prescription drugs at the time. Her preferred drug administration method was by enema. So it is possible that she received the fatal overdose in this form, perhaps administered by her housekeeper, Eunice Murray. This would explain the fact that there were few drugs in her bloodstream after her death. However, it seems unlikely that anyone would choose to murder her in this way.

The most plausible scenario seems to be that Monroe was indeed having an affair with the President, but was devastated when he broke the affair off and committed suicide as a reaction. Then, whoever discovered her dead body – whether it was her housekeeper or Robert Kennedy – panicked, moved things around in the room and delayed calling the authorities. Not a murder, then, but a scandal and a cover-up.

Finally, though, this is one of those cases where it seems unlikely that things will ever be conclusively proven either way. Suicide or murder? The choice is yours – and there are plenty of accounts out there to help you make your mind up.

THE ASSASSINATION OF MALCOLM X

At the time of his assassination on 21 February 1965, Malcolm X was one of the two leading black political figures in America. The other was Martin Luther King, who was himself assassinated just a couple of years later. However, where Martin Luther King was a broadly popular figure, a man of the church with a commitment to non-violent change, Malcolm was seen as a much more threatening figure. White liberals hailed Martin Luther King as the leader of the civil rights movement. On the other hand, Malcolm X was treated with suspicion because he was the main spokesman for a group called the Nation of Islam – commonly known as the Black Muslims – who were overtly anti-white and rather less inclined to turn the other cheek.

During the early sixties, Malcolm, a former petty criminal who had discovered the Nation of Islam while in prison, became a hate figure in the mainstream American media and was routinely vilified for his anti-white statements.

During the last year of his life, however, he began to travel more, especially to Africa, and after meeting anti-apartheid activists in South Africa he became convinced that black and white people could work together to achieve political change. This realization caused him

Malcolm X recognized the immense power of the press and used it assiduously in promoting himself and his organization the Nation of Islam.

to split with the Nation of Islam and during the summer of 1964 he formed his own group, the Organization of Afro-American Unity.

Shortly after forming this organization Malcolm X returned to Africa for a period of several months, finally returning to the United States in November 1964. While he was in Africa he continually complained that he was being followed by CIA agents. In Cairo he was seriously ill, perhaps as the result of having his food poisoned. Things were no better when he returned to the United States. Over the next few months a feud developed between Malcolm and the Nation of Islam, the group he had resigned from. Death threats were issued against him.

House firebombed

A week before his eventual assassination Malcolm's house in Queens, New York was firebombed. At the time Malcolm assumed that the Nation of Islam was behind the attack. The following day, 15 February, Malcolm made a speech at the Audubon Ballroom in Harlem. As he spoke a scuffle broke out in the audience. Six days later Malcolm returned to the Audubon. Mysteriously, all the other speakers that were scheduled to appear cancelled their engagements. While Malcolm was waiting to speak he allegedly confided to friends in the backstage area that he was not sure that it had been the Nation of Islam after all that had been behind the firebombing. Then he went onstage to give his speech.

At around 3.05 p.m. Eastern Standard Time a disturbance broke out in the crowd of 400. A man yelled, "Get your hand outta my pocket! Don't be messin' with my pockets!" Then a smoke bomb went off at the back of the auditorium causing confusion. Malcolm's bodyguards then moved forward to calm the crowd but meanwhile, taking advantage of the chaos, a black man came towards the stage and shot Malcolm in the chest at point-blank range with a sawn-off shotgun. Two other men quickly charged towards the stage and fired handguns at Malcolm. The three assassins attempted to escape, but the angry crowd managed to capture one of the two men with handguns, one Talmadge Hayer.

Malcolm's bodyguard Gene Roberts, actually an undercover cop, attempted to resuscitate

Malcolm X returning home on the 14 February 1965 after his house was firebombed. There were many suspects for the crime, but nothing was ever proven in court.

Malcolm but to no avail. Malcolm was dead. The autopsy was performed by New York City's Chief Medical Examiner, Dr Milton Helpern, and it was discovered that "the cause of death was multiple shotgun pellet and bullet wounds in the chest, heart, and aorta". Malcolm had been hit by eight shotgun slugs and nine bullets.

Malcolm's funeral was held in Harlem on 27 February 1965 at the Faith Temple Church of God in Christ (now Child's Memorial Temple Church of God in Christ). The ceremony was attended by 1,500 people. Malcolm X was buried at the Ferncliff Cemetery in Hartsdale, New York, where his friends took the shovels away from the waiting gravediggers and buried him themselves. Soon, three people were arrested for his murder. They were Nation of Islam members Talmadge Hayer, Norman 3X Butler, and Thomas 15X Johnson. All three were convicted of first-degree murder in March 1966.

On the face of it, this was an open and shut case, the result of infighting between black radicals. The Nation of Islam had murdered their greatest ex-member. The mainstream media either said good riddance or shed crocodile tears. And moved on. Gradually, though, suspicions began to circulate that all may not have been as it seemed.

A cover-up?

Suspicion centred around the notion that Malcolm might have been murdered by his fellow black men who had been manipulated: they could have believed that they were carrying out the wishes of the Nation of Islam.

It was not hard to find fuel for those suspicions. Even in the immediate aftermath of the murder a police source had told the *Herald Tribune* that "several" members of the highly secretive Bureau of Special Services (BOSS) were present in the audience at the time of the killing. One of those undercover cops, Gene Roberts, was one of Malcolm X's bodyguards at the time he was killed.

On 25 February 1965, four days after the assassination of Malcolm X, one of his senior lieutenants at the OAAU, Leon 4X Ameer, announced that he was convinced that his life was in danger. Less than three weeks later, he died of an apparent overdose of sleeping pills. It is alleged that he had been on the point of revealing evidence of government involvement in Malcolm's murder.

Further speculation surrounds the question of who really carried out the killing. Talmadge Hayer was certainly guilty, but there is plenty of evidence to suggest that his co-defendants were not even at the Audubon Ballroom at the time, and that the two other killers have never been brought to justice. As for Talmadge Hayer, he has stated that he was not a member of the Nation of Islam and "that the man who hired him was not a Muslim" either, according to a 1971 book, *The Assassination of Malcolm X*.

So was it the government or the Nation of Islam that was really behind the murder? There is a suspicion of government involvement here, and it is probably true to say that few people at the FBI shed many tears for Malcolm X. On the other hand, the Nation of Islam was locked in a struggle with Malcolm and its leading lights like Elijah Muhammad, and his eventual successor Louis Farrakhan did publicly call for Malcolm's elimination. It might well be that both parties are implicated. Perhaps the killers were Black Muslims and they were egged on by agents provocateurs. Whatever the truth behind the killing, the inescapable fact is that another great sixties leader was cut down in his prime, like John F. Kennedy before him and Martin Luther King not long afterwards.

THE DEATH OF DIANA, PRINCESS OF WALES

In the early hours of Sunday, 31 August 1997, news of the death of Diana, Princess of Wales, shocked the world. She and her lover Dodi Al-Fayed had been killed in a car crash as they sped through a Paris tunnel during the night. The driver of the car, Henri Paul, was also killed and Diana's bodyguard, Trevor Rees Jones, was seriously injured.

At first, the cause of the accident seemed straightforward enough. In an attempt to shake off the paparazzi who were pursuing the couple on motorcycles, the driver had taken the car down into the tunnel just a little too fast and had ended up smacking into one of the pillars inside it. But then, questions began to be asked. Why was the car travelling so fast? Had Henri Paul been drinking? If so, why had he been allowed to drive the car of Britain's number one celebrity, Diana, whose doomed marriage to the heir to the throne, Prince Charles, had generated pages of speculation and scandal in the worldwide press for over a decade. Why had the lights in the tunnel, and the security cameras, apparently failed just before the crash? Why had it taken so long for Diana, who was still alive after the crash, to be taken to hospital by ambulance?

And, after her death from cardiac arrest in the hospital, why was her body immediately embalmed, before a post-mortem could be undertaken? Had she been pregnant? Was it possible that MI6 and the British royal family wanted her – and her lover, son of one of Britain's richest businessmen, Mohammed Al-Fayed – out of the way? Had the Princess's indiscretions – her affairs, her criticism of the royal family, her increasingly eccentric behaviour – earned her enemies in high places? Al-Fayed senior claimed that the couple had been murdered, that they had been planning to marry and that the British establishment had

Diana pictured in 1996, the year before her death. She was relentlessly pursued by the paparazzi from the time of her marriage to the Prince of Wales in 1981.

decided that it was time to get them out of the way.

At first, Al-Fayed's claim was seen as paranoid but as time went on and more anomalies in the case surfaced, the theory began to seem less outlandish. Soon, others began to be convinced that this was no ordinary accident but a case of foul play.

Did MI6 kill Diana?

Initially, the press reported the tragic event as a car crash caused by the fact that Henri Paul, the driver, had simply made a mistake. But it then began to emerge that Paul, a security officer at the Ritz hotel, was an experienced and careful driver who had taken driving courses in the past. Not only this, but the car was only travelling at about sixty or seventy miles per hour, not at a hundred and twenty as had at first been reported. Next, there were allegations that Paul had been drunk at the wheel, but security cameras at the hotel showed that he was acting in a perfectly normal way minutes before taking the wheel. Moreover, he was unlikely to have been drinking when on call to such important hotel guests as Diana and Dodi Al-Fayed. Later, it was found that even before they took samples of his blood the police had in fact announced that Paul was drunk.

So, if the car was not going too fast and Paul was not drunk, why had the accident happened? Conflicting reports by some witnesses told of a car blocking the way so that Paul had to turn off his normal route into the tunnel and of cycles ramming the car as it travelled along, causing it to swerve. Some suggested that Paul had been in the pay of MI6, that he had been hired to kill Diana and Dodi and that something had gone wrong at the last minute so that he ended up killing himself as well. What was odd, and is still unexplained, is why Dodi asked Paul to drive the couple home instead of using his usual driver, Philippe Junot.

The fatal moment

According to some reports, all the lights in the tunnel went out shortly before the car approached, and the security cameras in the tunnel also failed. On this evidence, a theory has been constructed that Paul was used as a dupe, and that the French authorities deliberately arranged for the car to crash, thus killing the inmates. It has even been suggested that Rees Jones was somehow in on the plot because he survived, protected by his safety belt when Diana and Dodi were not wearing theirs. However, his involvement is somewhat implausible. Deliberately travelling in a car that is destined to have a fatal accident seems a little too risky a strategy – even for a man trained by the Parachute Regiment, one of the toughest regiments in the British army.

What does emerge as odd, however, is how the French authorities responded at the scene of the accident. In the immediate minutes after the crash, Diana appeared not to be seriously harmed. It later emerged that she was suffering from internal bleeding, but to the off-duty doctor who arrived first on the scene, Frederick Mailliez, she did not appear to be in a fatal condition. As she clearly needed medical attention, an ambulance was called but, strangely, it took over an hour to get to the hospital. It even stopped on the way for ten minutes! Afterwards, it was explained that the ambulance had stopped in order to administer a shot of adrenalin to the princess and that it had travelled slowly to avoid jolting her.

However, many remain unconvinced by this and they still cannot understand why Diana was taken to a hospital some distance away, when there were several nearby that could have attended to her. After all, this was no ordinary car crash victim. This was Diana, the Princess of Wales, one of the most famous and recognizable women on the planet.

Not only that, but important evidence was also cleared away from the scene of the accident immediately after the victims had been taken to hospital. Within just a few hours, the tunnel had been cleaned and disinfected and it was soon open to traffic once again. In normal circumstances, one would have expected the authorities to have sealed off the tunnel and have sifted through the evidence in order to find out exactly what had happened. But in this case they did not, which was curious.

The aftermath

Once Diana had died in hospital, the British royal family reacted oddly to the news. They reportedly sent an emissary to the hospital to retrieve any valuable family jewellery on the body. They then ordered the hospital to embalm the body right away, thus making it impossible for a post-mortem to be carried out. In particular, it was not possible to ascertain whether the princess had been pregnant or not. (She had apparently confided to Doctor Mailliez that she was.) When the press learned of the tragedy, the royal family were roundly condemned for not issuing an official statement and for failing to fly the palace flags at half-mast.

To this day, new theories are still pointing to the possibility that the top ranks of the British establishment joined in a conspiracy to kill Diana, Princess of Wales, because she had not only become an embarrassment to the royal family but also to the state in general. Other theories have also emerged, one of which is that she faked her own death so that she could disappear, thus avoiding the media circus that followed her everywhere she went. Perhaps we will never know the full truth.

What is clear, though, is that the circumstances of her death were not as straightforward as they at first appeared. Also, many of those who dealt with the accident, whether in Britain or in France, were guilty of incompetence, if not murder. In 2005 the official enquiry into Diana's death was reopened in France.

Mohammed Al-Fayed, father of Dodi, looks at the statue that he had commissioned of his dead son and Diana. Mr Al-Fayed is the main proponent of the Diana conspiracy theory.

THE JONESTOWN MASSACRE

Some events are so utterly bizarre and apparently inexplicable that conspiracy theories inevitably grow up around them, if only just to try and explain what on earth happened. One such event was the Jonestown Massacre, in which more than 900 people, all members of a cult living in a commune in Guyana, committed suicide by drinking Kool-aid laced with cyanide. Many of the dead were children who were given the lethal cocktail by their parents. Could it really be that they were all so much in awe of the cult leader, the Revd Jim Jones, that they willingly obeyed his order to commit suicide? Or were more sinister forces at work?

Before we can begin to answer that question we need to look at the facts of the matter. At the heart of whatever happened in Jonestown was the enigmatic figure of Jim Jones. Jones was born in Indiana in 1931. As a boy he became an avid member of a local Pentecostal church. By the time he was in his mid teens he had become a preacher, taking his message to the streets of Indianapolis, to both black and white communities. At the very beginning of his career his core values were apparently based around a sympathy with the underdog, regardless of race.

Nuclear war

Jones became a preacher at a Methodist Church in a white area and made a point of inviting black people to attend. By the late fifties he had his own church in Indianapolis, which he called The People's Temple. It ran programmes for the poor, including a soup kitchen, and his message of racial tolerance gained in popularity as the civil rights movement began to emerge. As he became increasingly critical of organized religion

Reverend Jim Jones preaching from the pulpit of the Preacher's Temple, Indianapolis.

he moved closer to a kind of revolutionary socialism.

The prospect of nuclear war was also becoming a worry to Jones and he conceived the idea of moving his congregation abroad to somewhere that would be safe from nuclear attack. From 1963 to 1965 he travelled around looking for such a place, while assistants ran his church. He spent time in Hawaii and Brazil and then, on his way back to the United States, he visited the newly socialist South American country of Guyana. Here, he thought, might be the perfect place for his new community.

Such a move would involve money that Jones did not yet have, so instead he moved his church to Ukiah, California, a place he believed to be relatively safe from nuclear attack. At first his church fared badly, with Jones himself becoming increasingly paranoid and dependent on prescription drugs. Following a

link with a much larger organization, however, the Disciples of Christ, his fortunes started to rise again. His following increased and he opened new churches in San Francisco and Los Angeles. Increasingly, his congregation was drawn from the poor black ghettoes. After Jones moved to San Francisco his church there was seen to be a real force for good and he became an influential political figure in the city during the early- to mid-1970s.

The jungle Utopia

In 1973, Jones began work on building his long dreamed of community in the Guyanese jungle. He named it Jonestown in his own honour. When, in 1977, his church, now with some thousands of members, came under investigation for tax evasion he made the decision to move his whole operation to Jonestown.

Bodies of followers of Reverend Jim Jones lie sprawled in death across the cult's compound in Guyana where they committed a mass suicide by drinking poisoned Kool-aid.

Just fifty members of the Peoples' Temple moved to Jonestown at first but by late 1978 the population had risen to over 1,000. In the early days it seemed that this was a genuinely Utopian story. Here was an interracial community living in harmony and supporting itself by agriculture. Gradually, though, reports began to leak out that all was not as it seemed. An article in the *San Francisco Examiner* on 13 November 1977 related the story of one Bob Houston whose father believed that he had been murdered when he had attempted to leave the Temple. Claims started to emerge that people were being held against their will at Jonestown. A local congressman, Leo Ryan, became interested in this story, all the more so when, in June 1978, he heard the testimony of Debbie Blakey, a defector from the community, who claimed that Jim Jones had led the population in rehearsals for a mass suicide.

Ryan decided that he had to investigate these alarming claims. On 14 November 1978, he flew out to Guyana along with his staff, a number of journalists and some concerned relatives. After some resistance from Jones and his aides, Ryan was finally allowed to visit on the evening of Friday 17th. Jones made sure that the community put on a show of unity but during the visit messages were passed to Ryan and the other visitors from people in the community who were anxious to leave.

Ryan told Jones that some people wanted to leave and he appeared to be happy for them to go. On the next day Ryan led a party of around twenty defectors to the nearby airstrip of Port Kaituma. Two light aircraft were to meet them and take them back to the Guyanese capital of Georgetown.

Cameraman filmed his own murder

On reaching the airstrip, however, one of the apparent defectors, thought to have been planted by Jones, turned a gun on his fellow members and shot and killed two of them. Then a truck and a tractor belonging to the Temple arrived and several armed gunmen opened fire. Ryan was shot dead, along with another defector and three journalists, including cameraman Robert Brown, who captured most of the awful events on film before being shot himself.

Meanwhile, back at the Jonestown compound, Jones had been tipped over the edge by the defections, even though he had initially appeared to take the news calmly. He called a meeting of the entire population and told them that these desertions marked the end of their Utopia and that the only thing to do was commit suicide. The meeting was recorded on tape and, amazingly enough, it is clear that most of those present agreed with Jones. Some members suggested that the children should be allowed to live but Jones overruled them and vats of poisoned soft drinks were brought out. The children were given their doses first: the poison was squirted into the mouths of the babies using syringes. The adults watched them die, then killed themselves.

Some did try to escape but they were faced with armed guards who shot at them. Many were killed, but over a hundred managed to escape into the jungle. Jim Jones himself died from a bullet in the head while sitting in his chair. It was presumably suicide. When outside helpers finally arrived they were greeted by a scene of unimaginable horror. Some 913 dead bodies lay there, many of them in orderly rows.

Mind control and the CIA

So was this simply an epidemic of madness – a classic story of a religious cult that had run out of control – or was there a hidden agenda behind the slaughter? It was not long before the first conspiracy theories appeared. The initial focus of suspicion, as is so often the case, was the CIA. Could Jonestown have been the site of a secret CIA mind-control programme that had just gone a bit too far? After all, the Jonestown settlement started up just as the CIA's notorious MKULTRA mind control programme was officially closed down. Could it have been revived illegally at Jonestown? The reason for the mass suicide, according to this theory, was that Leo Ryan had discovered the CIA's involvement during

Dead cult members amidst the debris of poison and Kool-aid cups used to adminster the poison.

his visit and the mass suicide was staged to cover it up.

If that seems breathtakingly cynical, it's nothing compared with the variant on this theory. This suggests that Leo Ryan was already on a CIA hit-list because of his sponsorship of the Hughes–Ryan Amendment which, if passed, would have required that the CIA report its planned covert missions to Congress for approval. According to this theory the real point of the events in Guyana was the murder of Leo Ryan – the mass suicide was simply staged in order to detract attention from this. However suspicious one might be of the CIA's involvement in covert activities though, the suggestion that they would be capable of murdering over 900 people in order to cover up the killing of a single man rather beggars belief.

In 1980, the House Permanent Select Committee on Intelligence investigated the Jonestown mass suicide and announced that there was no evidence of CIA involvement there. This, of course, failed to satisfy the conspiracy theorists and their case has been helped by the fact that the United States government has consistently refused to release any of the classified papers relating to the case.

Is it likely that the CIA really were involved in this appalling event? Probably not – or at least not in any instrumental role. The tape of the last speech made by Jones and the testimony of the survivors (many of whom still believe that Jonestown was at first a positive community) suggests that what happened at the end was after all a kind of collective madness, rather than a plot with any rational intention behind it. In some ways, the idea that the mass suicide happened for a purpose, rather than as a result of deranged behaviour on a grand scale, may be easier for us to accept – which is why conspiracy theories concerning the Jonestown Massacre continue to abound.

JOHN LENNON AND THE FBI

When John Lennon was murdered on 8 December 1980, the world reeled in shock. At the time of his death, Lennon was one of the most famous rock stars of all time and after a quiet period away from the public eye he was in the process of returning to the limelight with his first album in five years.

He was shot outside the Dakota Building, where he lived, by a young man named Mark Chapman who was obsessed by his hero and who had a history of mental illness. When Lennon arrived at the building that day with Yoko Ono, Chapman raised a gun and shot the star four times as he tried to run away. Lennon was rushed to hospital but died soon after his arrival. His death was mourned by thousands and he continues to be remembered by legions of fans.

The generally accepted view of the murder is that the mentally unstable Chapman acted alone, but there were also those who believed that Lennon was the

John Lennon pictured in 1969 during a "Bed-in-for-Peace", when he and Yoko Ono used the press attention surrounding their marriage to protest against the Vietnam war.

John Lennon poses with fan Paul Goresh on 8 December, 1980. Hours later, Lennon would be shot dead by Mark Chapman.

victim of a conspiracy and that Chapman had in fact acted under orders from a higher authority.

"Dangerous extremists"

During the late 1960s and the early 1970s, John Lennon had become unpopular with the United States government because of his outspoken criticism of the Vietnam war, among other issues. In a period when the counterculture was at its height, Lennon was seen as one of the most influential figures of the day and he was regarded by the government as highly subversive. J. Edgar Hoover of the FBI noted on Lennon's file that "all extremists should be considered dangerous".

As a result of the antagonism that arose between the star and the US authorities, Lennon was denied permanent residency in America and the administration was constantly looking for ways to deport him. By 1972, Lennon was known to be under surveillance and it was reported that he had spoken about fearing for his life and that of his family. He continued to be monitored by the FBI even when he retired from public life altogether, although less consistently.

Under the Carter administration, the authorities began to take less interest in the politically inactive Lennon, but when President Reagan was elected in 1980 all that changed. It so happened that Lennon emerged from his seclusion just as the new, right-wing administration was beginning to step up its anti-extremist tactics. To some, the fact that Lennon was murdered just a few months after he stepped into the limelight once more was highly significant.

Hard evidence

Although it is undoubtedly true that Lennon and his wife Yoko Ono were under suspicion from the United States administration for many years, there is a lack of hard evidence to link Mark Chapman to the FBI and the CIA. Several authors have suggested that government agencies brainwashed the insecure and mentally fragile Chapman, conducting "mind control" programmes on him that ordered him to murder John Lennon. However, while there is

plenty of documented evidence of Lennon's battle with the United States authorities in the shape of FBI files, those who claim that the government went one step further than mere harassment and had the star shot, using Chapman as the assassin, have very little in the way of facts to back them up. While the accounts of Lennon's constant run-ins with the authorities make fascinating reading – for a time, he was friendly with many of the leading lights of the United States counterculture, such as Jerry Rubin and Abbie Hoffman – it is difficult to see why the government would choose to resolve the conflict by having Lennon murdered. Even if they did, why and how they would have used Chapman to do the deed is another question.

Mind control

Several commentators have speculated that Chapman was specifically programmed to kill on command. They point to "Project Bluebird" and "Project Artichoke", the CIA's attempts to investigate the possibilities of using scientific methods to control the behaviour of their agents. "Mind control" experiments were conducted using a number of methods including hypnosis and drugs. Chapman, it is alleged, became a pawn in this game, a "Manchurian Candidate" who was cold-bloodedly programmed to go out and shoot Lennon for the security services.

The death of John Lennon at the hands of crazed "fan" Mark Chapman marked a new intensity of celebrity obsession. Here the London New Standard *reports on the killing that shocked the world.*

Could Mark Chapman have been a subject of mind control by the FBI and the CIA?

to commit the murder, the FBI would draw attention away from their own involvement in the crime. However, there are several problems with this theory, apart from the fact that there is so little hard evidence to support it. In particular, it seems unlikely that such a person would make a reliable hit man, to say the least. By the time of his death, John Lennon had made himself very unpopular with the powers that be, both as a result of his political pronouncements and his affiliations to left-wing groups. However, the idea that the CIA or the FBI decided to resolve the situation by programming a mentally unstable gunman to take potshots at him in the middle of New York does seem a little far-fetched.

The fact remains, though, that in 1980 John Lennon was re-emerging from a fallow period to become a public figure once again and that this coincided with a shift towards the right in American politics. Perhaps it was the case that the United States administration feared a re-run of the battles that Lennon had fought with the authorities in the past. Nevertheless, in the absence of hard evidence to link Chapman to the security agencies, it seems more likely that this was sheer coincidence and that, tragically, Lennon met his death just as his star was beginning to rise once more. Perhaps it is harder for many to accept that he was the unfortunate victim of a random killing than that there was a conspiracy to plot his murder.

Whether or not a person can, in fact, be trained to kill – particularly if this is against their wishes – is questionable. On the other hand, some psychologists have argued that where a subject has a deep-seated desire to kill, and has a specific target in mind, he or she may be encouraged to do so by using various persuasive techniques. This is, of course, especially effective where a subject already has a distorted sense of reality, as in the case of Mark Chapman.

Conspiracy theorists argue that by using a lone drifter with a history of mental illness

THE SHOOTING OF TUPAC AND BIGGIE

Rap star Notorious B.I.G., a.k.a Biggie Smalls, pictured here with label boss Sean "Puffy" Combs a.k.a P. Diddy. Many blame Smalls' shooting on the intense rivalry which existed between the East coast and West coast rap scenes.

During the early 1990s, rap became the biggest music in America and its leading artists not only started to appear in the pop charts but also in the news headlines. Increasingly, the new breed of rappers not only described the gangster life but they started to live it too. Two of the leading names in the world of gangster rap were Tupac Shakur and the Notorious B.I.G. (a.k.a. Christopher Wallace or Biggie Smalls).

Initially friends, they soon became sworn rivals. In fact, the two men seemed to be polar opposites. Tupac was based on the West coast while Biggie was based on the East. Tupac was signed to one leading rap label, Death Row, while Biggie was signed to its leading competitor, Bad Boy. Even their physiques were very different. Tupac was wiry and lean while Biggie, as his name suggests, was big all round. Both of them, however, were shot down in their prime, and the circumstances of their murders have kept the conspiracy theorists busy ever since.

Tupac was born in the Bronx, New York City on 16 June 1971. His given name was Lesane Parish Crooks but soon after his birth his mother Afeni, a member of the Black Panthers, changed his name to Tupac Amaru Shakur. He had a poverty-stricken, transient childhood in New York, before moving to Baltimore where he attended Baltimore School for the Arts during his teens and studied dance and theatre. However, when the family moved again, this time to Marin County, California, Tupac started to go off the rails and became embroiled in drug dealing. He also started getting seriously involved in rap music, making his recording debut in 1990. In the following year his acting training paid off when he won a lead part in the gangster film *Juice*. In the same year, 1991, he also released his first album.

Shot in the head and survived

All of a sudden Tupac was a star with a string of hit records and several more film appearances. At the same time, however, he became involved in a series of violent incidents. In one of these, in Oakland in 1991, Tupac was the victim of police brutality. In another he shot two policemen in Atlanta because he thought they were abusing a black motorist. Charges against Tupac were dropped, however, when the police officers were discovered to be intoxicated and in possession of stolen weapons. In December 1993 Tupac was charged with sexually abusing a woman in his hotel room and was subsequently sentenced to four years in prison. While still on remand, though, Tupac was shot five times by two men in a New York recording studio. He survived, despite being shot in the head and in a subsequent interview said that he believed that Biggie, who up until then he had considered a friend, and Biggie's label boss Sean "Puffy" Combs, were responsible for the attack.

In the following year, February 1995, Tupac began his prison sentence. He was released after eight months, when his own label boss Suge Knight put up $1.4 million bail. In return for this, however, Tupac had to agree to release three albums for Knight's Death Row Records.

The first of these albums, All Eyez on Me, sold more than nine million copies.

Disturbingly, the video for the single "I Ain't Mad at Cha", filmed a month before his death, showed Tupac being shot and killed. Immediately before his death Tupac recorded another album, The Don Killuminati: The 7 Day Theory, using the pseudonym Makaveli.

A prophetic album

The album was full of death-related imagery and it soon proved prophetic. On 7 September 1996 Tupac Shakur was hit four times in a drive-by shooting in Las Vegas, after watching a boxing match between Mike Tyson and Bruce Seldon. He died from the four gunshot wounds in the Las Vegas University Medical Center hospital six days later, on February 13th.

The Las Vegas police never found the culprits but they believed that Tupac's killers were Southside Crips. The evidence for this was that a few hours earlier Tupac had been involved in a fight in a hotel lobby with a 21-year-old Crip named "Baby Lane" Anderson. Anderson was interviewed by the police but not charged with the murder. Witnesses, unsurprisingly, were reluctant to come forward.

Within the rap world, however, suspicion soon fell on Biggie Smalls and Bad Boy records. Rumours abounded that Biggie had paid the Crips to kill Tupac. Suspicion intensified when Tupac's friend, Yafeu "Kadafi" Fula, who had been present at the shooting and was believed to know the killer's identity, was himself killed in an execution-style murder in New Jersey.

While the rumours about Biggie's involvement were not enough to cause the police to act, it came as no surprise to the public when, on 9 March 1997, just two years after Tupac's murder, Biggie himself was gunned down in Los Angeles when leaving a party given by *Vibe* magazine. Once again, the police were unable to find a witness who was prepared to come forward to identify the gunmen and the case remains unsolved. However, this time the suspicion fell upon Tupac's label boss Suge Knight.

So were the two fallen rappers simply victims of a gang culture that had run out of control or were their murders deliberately brought about by their rap music rivals? A story in the *Los Angeles Times* purported to prove that Biggie had ordered Tupac's killing, paid the killers, and provided them with the gun. The writer even alleged that Biggie had been in Los Angeles at the time. He did not explain, however, that no one had noticed the presence of the 6ft 3in 300lb rapper and his entourage. And in due course, clear evidence was produced to demonstrate that Biggie had been in a New York recording studio at the time of Tupac's death.

Rapper Tupac Shakur on stage. Shakur's shooting left the rap world shocked: it would be far from the last killing, however.

Worth more dead than alive?

Interest in the case was re-ignited in 2002 by the documentary "Biggie and Tupac", made by British film-maker Nick Broomfield. The film pointed towards a sensational conclusion – that Suge Knight might have been responsible for murdering his own artist, Tupac, and that he then killed Biggie in order to cover up the initial murder so that it would look like a revenge killing.

The motive for this, supposedly, was that Tupac was about to leave Death Row having discovered that Knight was cheating him of royalties. At that point Knight decided Tupac was worth more to him dead than alive (a theory borne out by the enormous success of Tupac's posthumous releases). This idea was backed up by an alleged prison confession by Knight to another inmate and also by Knight's long record of using violence to get his own way in business deals.

It is a neat theory but one with a lot of holes in it. For starters, Knight was sitting next to Tupac when the car they were in was sprayed with bullets. One bullet nicked Knight's head. It would have been an incredibly risky plan for Knight to execute. Secondly, if the murder of Biggie was committed in order to cover up the killing of Tupac, surely he would have carried it out sooner and not waited for two years. Also, Knight would inevitably have been a suspect in Biggie's murder.

That said, it is a lot more plausible than the other conspiracy theory that surrounds the case, which suggests that Tupac, like Elvis, is not dead at all. The evidence for this supposition is a familiar mix of song lyrics that allegedly point to Tupac having faked his own death, the fact that his last album cover had a picture of himself being crucified (Jesus was resurrected after his crucifixion) and his use of the name "Makaveli" for this last album. This was inspired by his reading of Machiavelli, who once wrote that faking one's death is a useful tactic for fooling one's enemies.

Fans have added on an ever more tenuous list of supposed clues to Tupac's "faked" death. However, they have a hard time gainsaying the evidence to the contrary that was provided by the 1997 publication of a leaked photograph showing Tupac's badly damaged corpse lying on an autopsy table.

BIBLIOGRAPHY

Noel Botham, *The Murder of Princess Diana*, Kensington Publishing Corporation, 2004.

Alexander Cockburn, Jeffrey St. Clair, *Whiteout: The CIA, Drugs and the Press*, Verso, 1998.

Richard J. Evans, *Telling Lies About Hitler: The Holocaust, Hitler, and the David Irving Libel Trial*, Verso, 2002.

Joachim C. Fest, *Inside Hitler's Bunker: the Last Days of the Third Reich*, Farrar, Straus and Giroux, 2004.

James H. Fetzer (ed.), *Murder in Dealey Plaza: What We Know Now That We Didn't Know Then*, Open Court, 2000.

Stewart Galanor, *Cover-Up*, Kestrel, 1998.

Devon Jackson, *Conspiranoia! The Mother of All Conspiracy Theories*, Penguin, 2000.

Barbara Leaming, *Marilyn Monroe*, Three Rivers Press, 2000.

Jim Marrs, *Inside Job: Unmasking the 9/11 Conspiracies*, Origin, 2004.

Michael Newton, *The Encyclopedia of Conspiracies and Conspiracy Theories*, Checkmark, 2005.

Dick J. Reavis, *The Ashes of Waco: An Investigation*, Syracuse University Press, 1998.

Michael Shermer, *Why People Believe Weird Things, Pseudoscience, Superstition and Other Confusions of Our Time*, Owl Books, 2002.

Jonathan Vankin and John Walen, *Eighty Greatest Conspiracies of All Time: History's Biggest Mysteries, Cover-ups and Cabals*, Citadel Press, 2004.

WEBSITES

http://www.alternet.org/ Alternative takes on current affairs.

http://www.coverups.com/ Entertaining site about the great cover-ups of history.

http://www.conspiracyarchive.com/ Material on the Illuminati, secret societies, mind control, etc.

http://www.crystalinks.com/roswell.html Information about the Roswell, New Mexico UFO/alien incident.

http://www.ufoevidence.org/ Site dedicated to UFO sightings, research, etc.

http://www.badastronomy.com/index.html For a sceptical, scientific view of conspiracy theories involving the moon landings, UFOs, etc, this site is hard to beat.

http://www.forteantimes.com/ Well-presented magazine concerning supernatural phenomena.

PICTURE CREDITS

INDEX